NOT GUILTY!

NOT GUILTY!

FROM CONVICT TO CHRISTIAN
THE JIM DYCUS STORY

JIM AND BARBARA DYCUS

1817

Harper & Row, Publishers, San Francisco

Cambridge, Hagerstown, New York, Philadelphia, Washington,
London, Mexico City, São Paulo, Singapore, Sydney

FIRST EDITION

Library of Congress Cataloging-in-Publication Data

Dycus, Jim.
   Not guilty!

   1. Dycus, Jim.   2. Converts — United States — Biography.   3. Narcotic addicts — United States — Biography.   4. Crime and criminals — United States — Biography.   I. Dycus, Barbara.   II. Title.
BV4935.D93A3   1988   248.2'46'0924   [B]   88-45133
ISBN 0-06-062103-6

88   89   90   91   92   HC   10   9   8   7   6   5   4   3   2   1

To the memory of my spiritual father, Ken Schmidgall, whose unconditional love and aggressive kindness to the old Jim Dycus demonstrated the power of God to remove my guilt and liberate me from my bondages.

And to George Cope, a man who believed in the new Jim Dycus enough to allow me the opportunity to fulfill the call of God upon my life to full-time service.

Contents

Preface

This book is the story of the man who, next to Jesus Christ, has had the most profound influence on my life.

Jim's life has challenged me from the first time I heard him tell of the transformation God had brought to pass. I had never met anyone like Jim before. Oh, I had met people whose lives had been dramatically changed by Christ, but never one so intensely committed to the Christ who changed him.

I had been a Christian all my life, but it was Jim who taught me what real faith is. I was in full-time ministry when we met, but he showed me the real meaning of dedication. I have been privileged to watch him grow up and mature into the man of God he is today. There is no man on earth whom I would rather have as head of my home, father to my children, priest of my family.

I am greatly honored to be able to introduce you to my husband, Jim Dycus. *Not Guilty!* is his life story. The story of Jim Dycus: fifteen-year heroin addict, criminal, alcoholic, and divorced man. *But* it is also the story of another Jim Dycus: loving family man, committed Christian, gifted teacher, pastor to hundreds of single adults, and nationally recognized Christian speaker. The man I know is the *new* Jim Dycus. The old one I have never met.

In fifteen years I have never seen anything in my Jim that appeared to be that other man. When we met, I could not believe that he had ever been the man he told me about, and I still cannot. God has completely removed every shred of evidence that he ever existed. I believe that there is no man better able to shout forth the message that God can set the captives free. Jim Dycus has been set free. God has declared him *NOT GUILTY.*

Barbara Dycus
Casselberry, Florida, 1988

NOT GUILTY!

Except for the following, all individuals in this book have been given fictitious names.

Real names include:
    Fran Dycus
    James and Clara Dycus
    Ken and Rowena Schmidgall
    George Cope
    Barb, Jimmy, Jackie and Dinah Dycus
    Jimmy Swaggart
    Scott Dycus
    Alex Clattenburg

Introduction

I remember a morning in the middle of the winter of 1972 when I stood in front of a mirror in a Salvation Army Men's Social Service Center dormitory bathroom. That morning I faced the reality of the man I had become.

I knew that nobody wanted me. Both my parents had died because of me. My sister slammed the door in my face every time I tried to make contact with her. Aunts and uncles refused to admit that I belonged in their family. Four exwives despised me. Four little children were being protected from the contemptible man who was their father.

Not even the hospitals, jails, and rehabilitation programs wanted me anymore. Or the men on the streets, the dopies who once had been my only friends.

As I looked in that mirror, the desperate loneliness of not being wanted permeated every fiber of my being. Every hope was gone. I didn't even want myself; I hated and despised the man I was.

I'd been handcuffed many times. I'd been bound in strait jackets. But the bondage that I felt that morning to the pain-filled memories of fifteen years of drug addiction thrust me beyond all hope into the very pit of hell.

Not Guilty! is my life story. It's the story of that man I've just described: fifteen-year heroin addict, criminal, alcoholic, and divorced man.

But on January 21, 1972, my life was changed. That day, when I cried out one more time for help, my simple cry introduced me to someone who *did* want me. I met Jesus Christ, the only one who had the power to set me free from all my bondages and declare me not guilty forevermore.

That day I began an incredible journey toward becoming all that God designed me to be. This book will share that journey. It will give hope to those burdened by the hopelessness of addictive lifestyles. It will show the reader the path to overcoming failure. It will give hope for restoration to those with broken lives. It will inspire others to begin a similar journey.

I once read the story of a slave girl who was being sold at auction. Two men were bidding. The price rose far above the cost of the other slaves at the auction block. Finally she was sold to the highest bidder. As she stood before him in fear, he held the bill of sale proving his ownership up in front of her, then ripped it into a thousand pieces.

"My dear," he said to her, "you're free! I bought you so that I could free you."

She fell to her feet before him. "Oh, master," she cried out in gratitude, "I'll love and serve you forever!"

The price Christ paid for my freedom has bound me to him for eternity. My desire is to love and serve him forever.

In *Not Guilty!* I've let you see where Jesus brought me from, and where I am today, to paraphrase the song lyric. The God I serve has taken me out of bondage to drugs, alcohol, crime, lust, divorce, guilt, loneliness, bitterness, anger, and rejection. His precious son, Jesus, paid the price of my freedom from slavery to sin in order that I might go free.

Baring my soul to you in this book has not been easy. In fact, it was the hardest thing I've ever done. I did it for you—to prove to you that God *can* break any bondage to sin.

I've been bound; I know how it feels. Satan bound me to my past, led me down a path of total destruction until I lay in the pit of hell, broken and despised by everyone I knew. Then he threw that past in front of me, not once but millions of times. The daily parade of pain that I endured for years—all the faces of the people I had hurt passing through my memory—bound me hopelessly to the evil, taunting control of Satan.

The problem I had wasn't heroin; it was Satan and his chains of sin. The single most important thing that I could share with you is the news that Satan doesn't hold those keys that lock you in your bondage. *Christ does!* When he died on that lonely hill of Calvary, he got off that cross and walked into the very pit of hell to confront Satan and grab the keys away from him. Then he used them to open my chains, *your chains*—to let the captives go free.

"If the Son therefore shall make you free, *ye shall be free indeed!*" (John 8:36, KJV).

God was able to completely eradicate all the bondages of my old life. Greater than that, he was able to take those bondages and turn them into stepping-stones to my greatest victories.

He took my loneliness and gave me a family. He removed my failure and allowed me to become pastor to hundreds of single adults. He broke my bondages and gave me liberty to preach the power of his grace and forgiveness throughout this nation.

My God has created me anew. He can do the same for you. *Not Guilty!* is the story of a man unhindered by his past—a man who knows, beyond the shadow of a doubt, that *there is no limit to what you can be if you allow God to make you anew too!*

1. The Homecoming

It was a bright, warm spring day in 1986 as I walked out to the mailbox in front of our home in Casselberry, Florida. I opened the door and looked inside. A personal letter lay on the top of the pile of bills and junk mail.

As I pulled the letter out of the mailbox, I glanced at the return address—*Tennessee!* My heart jumped: Tennessee meant family. I looked more closely and was shocked to see that the letter was from my Aunt Annie, Mom's older sister.

I stood there in front of the mailbox in our front yard as I ripped the letter open. I hadn't heard from Aunt Annie since Mom died. I opened the envelope and discovered that it was a form letter that began, "Dear relatives." The letter continued, "We are having a twenty-five-year reunion in July. Please plan to attend."

Twenty-five years from what? I wondered. A quick calculation gave me the answer. It was twenty-five years from July 1961, the month my Mom was hit by a train and killed instantly.

Except for my sister, Fran, and her family, I hadn't seen any of my relatives in twenty-four years. In fact, I hadn't even had any kind of contact with them for almost five years. Until my brother-in-law, Jack, found me in 1973 to tell me that my sister had died. That was the year Barb and I had married and put our names in the phone book.

But it had been a dream of mine to go back "home" for years. Even though I was only three when we moved to Chicago, that's what Tennessee is to me—my roots are there, and many of my childhood memories take place during happy summer vacations spent there—but the worst time of my life took place there too.

Barb and I planned to make the trip to Tennessee. As July got closer and closer, however, my anxieties about the trip grew greater.

"I wonder if I'll recognize anybody," I said to Barb, "or if anybody will recognize me?"

Deep inside I was afraid they would. How would they act toward me? After being gone so long, how would I feel? I wondered. Would

I be able to control my emotions, or would I again have those terrible flashbacks of the past—that nightly parade of pain-filled memories?

July arrived, and Barb and I and our kids—Jimmy, Jackie, and Dinah—started our trip. After spending a few days in North Carolina, we turned our borrowed van west, toward Tennessee.

Jimmy, my seven-year-old son, sensed my apprehension. From his position in the passenger seat, where he was "riding shotgun," he looked over at me and smiled.

"I'll bet this will be the best vacation in our whole life, Daddy," he reassured me.

I glanced at Jimmy. I couldn't help smiling back as I thought how much like me he was. Even his teeth looked like mine used to when I was seven. "He's your clone," Barb once said.

"Someday trips like this will be very meaningful to you, Jimmy." I said to him. "Just like when my daddy was taking me places." I reached over and patted his leg. "I liked to be with my Dad," I explained.

"Just like I like to be with my dad!" he eagerly responded.

At the mention of my father, the memories of a broken past flooded back to me. Facing those memories by taking this trip was one of the greatest challenges of my life. I had been avoiding this for almost twenty-five years. And avoidance is so contrary to the way that I usually deal with difficult things. I am a confronter; I like to face tough things head on, deal with them, and overcome them.

We had divided our trip into two minitrips. The first part we planned to spend in McKenzie, Aunt Annie's hometown, where the reunion was to take place. The second phase would take me home to Newburn, where my parents are buried.

It was after dark when we drove into McKenzie, a tiny Tennessee town nestled in the hills. As we came up over the hill into the southwest end of the town, I remembered driving with Mom and Dad to visit Aunt Annie and Uncle Lester. The little town looked almost the same. The saloon still stood on the same corner where we had passed it every time we came to visit, and farmers' pickup trucks still filled the parking lot. Little white frame houses lined the half-dozen or so streets that formed the town. As we sat at a stoplight, I remembered all the other landmarks too, and recognized the street angling off to the left toward the old farm Aunt Annie had maintained until she moved into town a few years earlier.

"Will Uncle Jack be there, Daddy?" Jimmy wanted to know as we pulled into the motel parking lot.

"Yes, and a lot of other relatives you've never met," I answered, suddenly very shaky about the dozen or more cars I saw. I was sure that they belonged to family members I would be seeing for the first time in many years. So many things have happened since then, I thought.

Jimmy recognized Jack, who was walking toward his room, and bounded out of the van to run and see him. After greeting Jack, Barb took the sleepy, grumpy girls into our room to get them ready for the sack.

"Let's go, Jimmy," Jack said to me. "Everyone's down at Aunt Edith's room." Aunt Edith is my mother's younger sister.

As I glanced toward the motel door where he pointed, my apprehension broke out into a full-fledged case of nerves. My palms felt clammy and my knees shaky—just like my insides.

"Well, it's here," I said to myself. "The next step of my twenty-five-year journey will be when I step into that room!"

So many things were going through my mind. For years I'd wondered how my relatives felt about me. I hadn't even been able to go to Dad's funeral because of my addiction. I knew some of what they had thought years earlier: they had encouraged their children—my cousins—to stay away from me, fearing that I'd lead them astray into the same wild life I was living.

I was so glad Jack was with me now. He'd known me through the worst of my past, and yet he had accepted me back into his life. His daughter, my niece, was there too, with her husband. It had been a special joy of mine to unite Nancy and Steve in marriage a few months back. They had been able to forgive me my past.

But what about those in that motel room?

Just then the door opened. I immediately recognized Aunt Annie over in a chair in the corner. As she saw me, she stood to her feet, and with arms outstretched grabbed me in a hug. "Oh, Jimmy, we're so glad you're back!" she said, tears streaming down her face. The others began to do the same. I was overcome with the emotion of their acceptance. One of them said to me, "Oh, your mom and dad would be so proud of you today, Jimmy, if they could only see you!"

That three-day time of restoration with my family was a wonderful experience. Everyone was thrilled that "little Jimmy" had come back home. We renewed acquaintances, caught up on old times, and met new family members. I discovered that no one really knew the details of my long absence — yet even as those missing details were revealed, I felt loved and accepted. It felt good to be part of a family after so many lonely years.

But I knew that the journey hadn't ended yet; McKenzie was only a rest area on my way home. The toughest miles still lay ahead. The second part of our trip would take us back to Newburn: my parent's home, the place where they were buried, and the town where all the pain began for me. I still wasn't sure I could do it — face again all those memories.

"Let's go out where Aunt Annie's farm used to be before we leave McKenzie," I said with a smile to Barb. "I've promised the kids that they can do some climbing."

As we turned off the highway onto the dirt road leading to the farm, I saw the hills ahead. "There they are, Jimmy — there are my 'mountains.'"

"Yeah! Can I go climb them, Dad?" he called to me as he hurled himself out of the car.

As I watched him eagerly heading for the hills, I was a boy again. I remembered the happy summers when we would travel from Chicago to Aunt Annie's farm. I spent hours every day playing on these hills. I worked my way all the way to the top and then slid down the deeply rutted slopes, ending up in a pile of loose red dirt on the bottom. I imagined all sorts of adventures on those hills. I was an army general leading my troops up them to capture the enemy fort on the top. I was a mountain climber, risking my life to climb Mt. Everest, or an outlaw sneaking up to grab the unsuspecting traveler's gold. Aunt Annie's dogs would always come along with me, and we all tumbled down the red dirt hills until we were covered with dirt too.

Barb's voice brought me back to the present. "Mountains?" she asked with a laugh. The hills were only twenty feet high!

Jimmy came running back over to us, having already been to the top of the nearest hill. "Hey, Dad, I thought you said they were big!" he chided me.

"Well, son, when you're a kid, things look so big. I know these hills looked a lot bigger to me back then. But when you come back twenty years later, somehow they don't look so big at all. The challenges of life are the same. When we're trying to do things, they seem big, and hard, and tough. But after we do them, they seem awfully small." I wasn't sure I was saying this for his benefit or for my own. I patted Jimmy on the shoulder. "Remember that, son. Anything we do is like that!"

Just then Jackie came running up covered with red dirt. I laughed. "That's just the way I used to look!" I told her, as we walked down the dirt road to where the farmhouse used to stand.

We piled back into the van and headed west again toward Newburn. On the way we stopped in nearby Dyersburg to see the ballfield where I had played shortstop four or five nights a week in my early twenties. As we drove, I told the kids more about my early summers in Tennessee. I shared the happy memories, back when I was a boy and life was full of fun. But soon pain-filled memories of those later years crowded out the happy ones, and I began to drive in silence. "God, help me do it," I silently prayed.

I thought about those ballgames I used to play at Dyersburg as a young adult. My parents, who had left Tennessee when I was three, had moved back down to try to hold their lives together. I'd followed, trying to get away from the bondage of drugs in Chicago. But none of us had been able to recapture happiness; in fact, that time of life became a nightmare for us all.

"Here's the ballfield, kids!" I recognized the old stands, and the same scoreboard was still there. I could almost see my team standing there, waiting for me to join the play. Suddenly, as I walked out on that field, everything was exactly the same as it used to be! The memories rushed back in torrents, and the tears rolled down my cheeks.

If only I could have started my life over from here, I thought. If only I could have kept my head clear from here, I could have had a professional ball career.

"Hey, Dad, look what I found!" Jimmy called excitedly as he ran to join me on the field. I looked at the baseball in his hand and the hat on his head. I was reminded that life goes on. Boys still play baseball, and men still mess up their lives. But God is still on his throne. He still wants to liberate those bound by Satan.

"Pitch it to me, Jimmy," I yelled back to him.

Later, as we walked arm in arm off the field, I looked down at Jimmy. "Daddy felt like he was twenty-one again, son!"

As we pulled away from the ballfield and headed toward Newburn, we passed a spot where the road forked. It was there that I had knocked a lamppost down with my car so many years ago. I remembered my drunken despair that night long ago. Now, as I glanced in my mirror and saw a police car pull out on the road behind us, the memories rushed back again and I was filled with anxiety about what lay ahead.

The downtown square at Newburn looked the same. I pointed out some landmarks to Barb and the kids: "There's the old church Mom and Dad attended; there's the jail on the right, and the grocery store is over there. The pool hall where I used to hustle pool is gone."

We turned to the right, and I pulled the van over to the curb.

"Why did you stop, Jim?" Barb asked.

"There they are—the tracks!" I told her, staring straight ahead. "The graveyard is about a half-mile down the road."

I sat in silence, staring straight ahead. My hands clenched the steering wheel as I tried to calm the raging torrent of emotion welling up within, my knuckles white from my grip on the wheel. I knew the time had come. "I think I'll go walk it," I said.

Barb didn't respond, realizing just how private my pain was at that moment. So much hurt had been buried deep inside me for so many years. She knew that I had to dig the hurt up—and cast it off—here, on these railroad tracks where Mom had died.

I walked the 50 feet or so up to the tracks, but I couldn't turn. I couldn't stand to look down the tracks—down the 1,500 yards to where Mom had died.

I whirled around and walked back to the van. "Let's go to the graves first," I said to Barb.

"This is the street where Daddy used to live," I said to the kids. "See it? There's our house!" Our white frame house still looked the same as it did when we had lived there years before. I stopped the car just before the house to point out the little side window of the room that used to be my bedroom. The sloping roof that overhung the porch still looked sway-backed. I also showed the kids the path out back that led first to the old outhouse and then on down the hill to the railroad tracks.

"Hey Dad, there's the cemetery!" Jackie called out.

I needed no reminder. It stood right across the street from the little house. I pulled the van into the cemetery drive and stopped. We could see most of the headstones from the car. Barb and I read the names, looking for the ones I knew were there. We didn't see them. Just as I was about to jump out to walk around I saw them.

As I walked over to the graves, tears flowed down my cheeks. I stood in front of their stones but couldn't bring my eyes to rest on the words. I knelt in the grass in front of the first and thought of Mom. A fragile, small woman, she'd spent her days working hard to care for her family. The second-eldest of nine children, she'd never known any life but hard work.

"Oh, it hurts!" I cried out loud. "I wish you could see me now, Mom and Dad. You never saw your prayers answered."

Suddenly the pain left. At that moment I felt free, light; it didn't hurt any longer. I'd been in front of Mom's grave many times before. For months after her death I had come every night, carrying a folding chair to her headstone, where I would sit and beg forgiveness from her silent grave. But I'd never felt this way before.

"Look, Ma, no folding chair!" I said.

As I looked over at the neighboring marker, I saw my father's name. I suddenly realized that I hadn't known the date he died.

"Barb, come here quickly!" I called. She hurried over, and I pointed to Dad's name.

"Do you see it?" I asked. I saw her smile and knew she understood.

"What're you looking at, Dad?" Jimmy wanted to know.

"The day my Dad died, Jimmy," I explained. He died on January 21, 1970. It was two years later *to the day* that I found the Lord!

My mind filled with memories of my dad. I remembered happy boyhood years. Dad and I had been so close then. I thought about how proud I'd been to walk hand in hand down the street with him. I closed my eyes and saw him standing before me. Tall and slim, his back straight, his shoulders back, he reached up to pull his fedora down to his thick, dark brows. With the ever-present cigarette dangling from the side of his mouth, he reached down to adjust my tie; then he slapped me on the back.

"There are four things I want you to never forget, son," he said gruffly to me. "Always comb your hair, brush your teeth, shine your shoes, and keep your fingernails clean!" Those childhood admonitions had stayed with me even through the bad years, and they're near-obsessions even today.

Dad's growing-up years had been terrible for him. His mother had died when he was a very young boy. His father had married again, this time to a woman who had three young boys of her own. She treated Dad horribly. He slept in the hay loft of the barn while her three boys had nice soft beds in the house. When she fixed her boys chicken and dumplings for supper, Dad ate bread and milk. Her boys went to school while Dad stayed home and worked the fields. She never spoke kindly to Dad, but rather did her best to make him feel incompetent and unloved.

I still don't understand why his father permitted this kind of treatment. He was a pretty strong-willed man, but many times he'd give in to her just to keep her quiet. Mom and Dad never talked about those things. They kept it away from us; they seldom mentioned bad things about other people.

When Dad had his own "little Jimmy," he couldn't bear the thought of ever doing anything to make me sad. He wanted me to have all the things he'd missed out on. He gave me anything I wanted. My sister, Fran, who was twelve years older than I, said that I was "his spoiled little brat."

As I sat there by Dad's grave, other, darker memories began to crowd out the happy boyhood years. I struggled to push them out, but as I reached for Dad's loving hand it seemed as though each memory pushed us further from each other. Finally a great gulf of emptiness separated us, and I realized that I could barely remember how he looked. The closeness that we'd shared was gone — only emptiness remained.

At least we share this day, I thought. I'll never have to grieve the anniversary of his death without being able to celebrate the start of my new life in Christ!

"Thanks, God," I silently prayed. "I needed that today."

After a moment I said to Barb, "It's time to walk the tracks." We got back in the van and drove to the place where I had stopped before.

I began my solitary walk down the tracks amidst a rush of memories. For years after Mom's death I wasn't able to even look at a train. It was only by the grace of God that I now could put one foot in front of the other, each step bringing me closer to the place.

"I can't remember exactly where it is, but I will," I said to myself. "When I get there, I'll know. *I'll know*," I said with quiet conviction. I walked on, further than I knew I should. "I've passed the place. I'm going to have to walk back," I thought aloud.

I told myself that I wanted to be sure this really was the place. But deep within I knew that I was only trying to postpone the inevitable moment of pain. I had been dreading this moment for twenty-five years. I had never been able to take this walk before. This 1,500-yard walk down a lonely set of railroad tracks had kept me bound to pain for twenty-five years!

Now at last I was there—about to face my Gethsemane.

I knew it was only because my Lord had faced his Garden of Gethsemane that I could face mine. For the first time I understood how he must have felt. I felt his agony and I knew his pain as he cried, "Father, let this cup pass from me. Nevertheless, not my will but thine be done" (Mark 14:36, paraphrase).

I knew those were his words, but—oh, my Lord—that day they were also mine!

"I'm about 200 yards away, but I know where I'm going," I said aloud. "Yes, I'm going to the place. It's almost over. I never thought I'd be coming back here; I never thought I could stand the pain."

Suddenly I was there! My feet stopped of their own accord and I felt as though a cage had dropped down and closed me in it. I stood still at exactly the spot where Mom had died so many years before. But again, as at the graves, even though I stood there I felt removed, free from the pain of being there, liberated from the guilt of knowing that it was I who made her step onto those tracks in front of that train.

"It's over! Thank you, Jesus, it's over!" I cried.

As I started back down the tracks toward where Barb and the kids were waiting, I knew that I was walking out of my pain and into the freedom Christ had given me. I spoke aloud: "Therefore, if Jim Dycus be in Christ, he is a new creature: old things are passed away; behold, all things are become new!" (2 Corinthians 5:17, KJV).

I turned to look back at the spot once more and saw, lying beside the rail, a rusty railroad spike. As I bent to pick it up, I realized that just as the railroad tie had loosened its grip on that old spike, *so God had loosened the hold that guilt had kept on me for so many years.*

I stood looking at that rusty old spike, turning it around and around in my hands. Corroded, dirty particles began to fall to the ground in the twisting and rubbing of my hands. Each falling bit of rust became a memory, and I began to live again the years gone by. Painful memory after painful memory fell from me in the gentle, loving touch of God's hands at work forming a new creation of the Jim Dycus I used to be.

I could face the memories now, assured that as I relived them one more time they would fall away, never to corrode my mind again.

2. His Father's Son

My dad and I were buddies in those days — *big buddies!*

"Hey, Jimmy, come on down to the corner with us," my friends called as they rode by on their bikes, down the street we lived on in Chicago.

"Can't," I shouted back. "Me and Dad are gonna play ball as soon as he gets home."

I watched them ride away, then tossed my ball up in the air over and over as I sat waiting for my dad. Every time I caught it, I looked up the street to the corner that I knew he'd come around.

"C'mon, Dad, hurry up!" I said out loud.

My ball rolled out into the street and I jumped up to get it. Just then I saw Dad's car coming down the street. I threw my hat up in the air, shouting, "C'mon, hurry up, Dad!" as he pulled in the driveway.

"Just give me a minute, Jimmy," he said, rolling up his window.

I grabbed his glove off the step beside me and tossed it to him as he climbed out of the car. His hat fell off as he reached for the glove. Dropping his lunchbox down on the step and letting his cigarette butt fall to the sidewalk, he raced me to the curb for the ball. He got to it first and picked it up as I bumped into his legs. He grabbed me around the waist to lift me up and swing me around before letting me fall on the grass beside the curb. I jumped to my feet.

"Hey, run down there and catch a few," he said, pushing me down the street.

I caught the ball he threw and tossed it back to him. "Throw it harder, Jimmy," he called. "Someday you're going to play pro ball!"

Every night we played ball. He'd hit ground balls and fly balls for me to catch, and he taught me how to throw curve balls and screw balls. "Straighten out your finger," he'd tell me. "Now turn your wrist to the left a little when you throw."

Over and over we practiced. "Get it right, Jimmy. You can do it!" he'd tell me. The more he cheered me on, the harder I tried. With his encouragement I got better and better at the game.

If only Dad and I could have captured those moments together, we might have been able to take them out and release them later — as our relationship grew worse and worse. But neither of us suspected that anything could happen to destroy the special bond we felt for one another.

One night as he drove down the street toward where I was waiting, I could see that he was dangling something out the window. "Hey, Jimmy," he called, "go try them out." He waved a pair of shiny black spike shoes — the ones I had wanted for a long time.

I grabbed them, sat down, and yanked off my old tennis shoes. Rubbing my hands over the smooth black leather, I put those new spikes on. They felt so good on my feet! I saw a spot of dirt on one of them and wiped it off with my shirt.

"They fit, Dad, they fit!" I shouted, jumping up and down on the grass. I ran across the yard, feeling those spikes grab the ground with each step I took.

I tugged on his arm. "C'mon, Dad, throw me some balls to hit."

He laughed and let me drag him along by the arm to the empty lot on the corner. I ran with my bat to the back corner. "Throw it, Dad, throw it!" I shouted back to him.

"Okay, Jimmy, hit a home run," he called. I hit that ball as hard as I could and took off running.

"Hey, this is neat," I yelled as I ran to the old stump we used for first base. When I saw Dad catch the ball and come running to our third-base tree to tag me, I decided to slide in as I'd slid a thousand times before.

I stuck my legs out in front of me and slid to the ground. Those spikes stuck in the grassy dirt and jerked me back. I somersaulted over my feet and landed face down in the dirt, far from the base. My knees were skinned and bleeding and dirt was in my nose and eyes — even in my mouth. I spit it out as I slowly got up and wiped my face on my T-shirt.

Dad roared with laughter. "Can't slide that way now, son," he said. "You gotta do it different with those shoes. Put your right leg underneath your left and bend it so your toe leads. Then let your left leg slide along the top of the ground. Don't let it get caught in the grass."

I remember the first time I tried it. Sure enough, I put that leg underneath and slid all the way to base. I never had any trouble after that.

After several practice slides we heard Mom calling us. "James, Jimmy, come on home for supper."

Dad put his arm around my shoulders as we walked home. I hung onto his waist and skipped along beside him. "Jimmy, you keep practicing and one of these day you're going to play professional ball," he said. And I believed him. Years later I would long to feel his arm around my shoulder, hear him encourage me: "You can do it, son, you can do it."

As I sat down next to Dad at the kitchen table, he winked at me, put his arm over the back of my chair, and said, "Aren't you going to tell your mom about your new spikes, son?"

I laughed and told her all about how much better I could play ball with my new shoes. "I'll get a home run every time now, won't I, Dad?" I said, shaking his arm as I talked.

Dad laughed. "Sure will, son. You sure will," he answered.

Mom laughed too. "Your dad is so proud of you, Jimmy. You're exactly what he wanted. You're just like him!" she said, smiling at both of us. That smile would fade as time went on.

Dad and I shared more than our love of baseball. We went everywhere together while I was growing up. "Hey, Jimmy, come on, let's go," he would call, and I would jump in the car, ready for anything.

Every weekend we went fishing. We left on Friday night and drove across the city to the Fox River. We slept in the car and woke up early Saturday morning to fish.

"Hey, Jimmy, run up to the store and get some worms," Dad would say, nudging me awake. Instantly ready to go, I'd take off up the hill on my errand, returning with a pail of worms.

By the time I got back to the car, Dad usually had our fishing gear all laid out on the ground. We'd pick it up and trudge down to the river's edge, sitting down on our camp stools.

Hour after hour Dad could sit there, smoking endless cigarettes and throwing out his line again and again.

"Hey, Dad, I don't have nothin' to do," I'd finally tell him.

Laughing, he'd toss me some pocket change. "Run on up to the store again and get a candy bar."

So I'd wander along the river's edge, talking to the other fishermen and idly picking up what treasures I could find along the path.

Sometimes when I wandered back to Dad I found him sound asleep, stretched out on the bank with his ever-present felt hat pulled down over his eyes.

"Hey, Dad, I thought you came to fish," I'd tease, splashing water over him.

When the afternoon sun began to move behind the tall oak trees along the bank, I'd beg him to go home. "C'mon, Dad, we've been here long enough." I knew Mom would have a big supper waiting, and by then I was always starved.

"Okay, let's load up the car," Dad would say, picking up all the gear.

By the time we turned the corner onto our street, my mouth was always watering in anticipation. "What do you think Mom cooked?" I'd ask.

Smiling, Dad would say, "Run on up and see while I unload."

I'd bound up the steps to our second-story apartment two and three steps at a time, stopping long enough to growl at Skippy, our neighbor's feisty dog.

"Hey, Ma, I'm hungry. What's for supper?" I'd call as I opened the door. As soon as I walked in the warm kitchen, I'd smell the food cooking—often the smell of chicken baking and beans cooking on the stove. My mouth would water and my stomach growl. More than once (more than 100 times?) I reached for the plate of warm corn-bread sitting on the table.

Mom would see my hands and grab my arm, pulling it back and wrinkling up her nose at me. "Just as soon as you wash that fishy dirt off your hands, you can have some."

We'd sit down to a table covered with cornbread, beans, and chicken, and I'd eat until my stomach hurt.

"Jimmy, did you get the coal yet?" Mom would ask as night fell. Every night when the weather got cool, I had to go down into the basement and bring up two buckets of coal for the coal stove that warmed our house.

"Not yet," I'd tell her if I knew there was no way to get out of the job. Usually, though, I just disappeared about that time, and Dad or she would have to go for the coal.

"Time to go get it!" she reminded me if I hadn't made my escape.

I'd pick up the two buckets and head for the basement. At the foot of the steps was a gate leading into the neighbor's yard. On the other side of the gate sat Skippy. He was an ugly little dog, and he was mean! He was always there, growling at me every time I passed.

Every night Skippy and I had a little game we played. I'd get down on all fours and growl ferociously at him through the crack in the gate—a crack just big enough for him to stick his nose through. He'd lunge at the gate, barking and growling and trying to reach me. I always stayed close to the gate — talking to him, teasing him, egging him on. I'd even hit his nose with my hand every time he lunged at the gate.

The more I'd tease him, the madder he'd get. Soon I'd tire of the game, however; I'd pick up my coal buckets and head back up the steps. As I walked past Skippy one last time, I usually kicked the gate as hard as I could, snapping back at him, "Ain't *nobody* tougher than Jimmy Dycus!"

3. The Ninth Inning

We moved from Tennessee to the northside of Chicago when I was only three. When I was ten years old we moved from the North Side to the South Side of Chicago. After the move we lived in "Little Italy," a neighborhood Al Capone had made famous in the thirties. Even now it was still primarily an Italian neighborhood, and many members of the Mafia still lived there. More important, it was a neighborhood that loved its baseball.

Baseball had become my life. Dad and I still practiced every night. Only now, a couple of years after the move, it was usually a warm-up to a game. I was playing on a team known as the Midgets. We were one of the youngest teams in the neighborhood—at twelve, I was the youngest player—but we were also one of the best. We played teams much older than most of us.

"Jimmy, I'm so proud of you," Dad still told me. "And at least once a week: "You're going to play pro ball."

"Watch out for this guy, Jimmy," David called as the big kid walked up to the plate. "If he hits a ball past you, the game's over!"

I braced my feet, squatting down enough to keep the late-afternoon sun out of my eyes. It was the bottom of the ninth, and the score was tied. Worst of all, the bases were loaded. If this guy got a hit, chances were the opposition would score a run and we'd lose the game.

"Don't worry, he's not gonna put one past me," I muttered, teeth clenched and perspiration dripping down my face. I sounded a lot more sure of myself than I really was, though. This guy was known to be the best line-drive hitter in the area. Standing out there in my shortstop position, facing that big brute on the other team, I felt as if I'd made it to the big league.

His first five pitches were two strikes and three balls. This was it: either I got him, or he was going to do our whole team in. It all depended on me! He hit a line drive straight at me, but it was high enough that I knew I had to get back in the field if I was going to catch it. I ran back, keeping my eyes on the ball. My hat fell to the ground, and I squinted into the low sun. The only things that existed at that moment were me and that ball. I didn't think I was going to get it; it was still too high. As I reached up and jumped at the ball, I felt the familiar feel of leather hitting pigskin and I breathed a sigh of relief. By the time my feet hit the ground, the people in the stands were on their feet.

My teammates rushed over to me. "All right, Jimmy, you did it again!" they yelled, picking me up and swinging me around. Man, I felt good!

I loved the tension and thrill of a good ballgame. Soon, though, my restless nature became interested in more than baseball. Baseball was great, but once I'd conquered it, it seemed that I needed a bigger challenge.

One day after we finished practicing baseball in the parking lot of a huge warehouse, we noticed several big trailers near the unloading docks. I decided to investigate more closely.

"Watch out, Jimmy," my friend called. "They might have put the guard dogs out already!"

But the possibility of danger only made me want to get closer. I snuck up to the side of one of the first trailers. After making sure of my escape route, I whistled softly. Better find out now if those dogs are loose, I thought.

Nothing happened. It was too early for the dogs, yet late enough that the docks were empty of employees. The coast was clear.

I checked the door of that first big trailer. It was securely locked. I then walked along the line of trailers, checking each one until I came to one that someone had forgotten to lock. Looking around to be sure I was alone, I carefully opened the door enough to sneak inside.

At first I thought the trailer was empty. As my eyes adjusted to the dark, however, I saw that there were several large packages up in the front. I ran up and grabbed one, finding that I could carry it easily. By now I was scared to death that someone was going to catch me. But I liked the feeling.

Carefully I snuck back out the door and closed it, then crept back down the line of trailers until I reached the first one I had tried.

All I gotta do now is run across the lot to the hole in the fence and then over to those trees, I thought. All the way to the fence I imagined that the dogs were chasing me. It wasn't until I fell down on the grass beneath the trees that I dared to look around.

I was safe. No one had seen me.

Hey, nothing to it, I thought. I ripped the package open to see what I had risked my life to get.

"Nothing but some dumb old drapes!" I said angrily. "But it was still worth it. That's more fun than playing catch."

About that time I heard my mom's voice from down the street, calling me home. I didn't dare take those drapes home, so I just left them there under the trees. I couldn't wait to tell Jason and Paul what I'd done.

I liked the thrill of doing things I wasn't supposed to do, and I liked the way my buddies talked about the crazy things I did. They always got in trouble with their parents when they did something wrong, but I never did. That gave me the edge, and I liked being recognized as the tough kid on the block.

Across the alley from our house was a morgue. My friends and I used to watch the big black hearse as it brought dead bodies to the morgue. We knew that many times there were two or three bodies stored inside, and we imagined how the people had died.

Right next to the morgue was a big telephone pole with climbing stakes at the top. Someone had told us that if you could get up that pole to the stakes, from the top of the pole you could easily jump onto the roof of the morgue. And from the roof you could see through the glass skylight to where they lined up all the dead bodies.

Jason and I decided to make that climb, but there didn't seem to be any way to reach the first stake on the pole. For weeks we tried to figure out a way. "Hey, Jason, this is it! I've got it," I shouted excitedly to him one day as we passed an empty lot.

"What do you mean?" he asked.

"Look what someone threw away," I told him, pointing to an old stepladder. "Now we can reach the stakes on the pole."

We dragged the stepladder home with us. The next day was Saturday, and the morgue was closed. Perfect. We met outside my house early in the morning.

"Come on, let's hurry before everyone gets up, I suggested. Grabbing the ladder, we carried it across the alley and propped it up against the pole.

"Hold it while I try," I said to Jason.

I hurried up the ladder to the top. It was too short; I *still* couldn't reach the first stake.

"Now what?" Jason asked as I came back down the rungs.

I thought a minute. We'd tried so many times before that I wasn't about to give up this time.

"The wagon!" I shouted. "Go get my old wagon."

Jason ran across the alley to my house. He quickly grabbed my old wagon from under the back stairs and came running back. We put it by the pole and set the ladder in it.

"Hang on, Jason," I said.

"It's not gonna work, Jimmy," he told me. "You're gonna fall."

"Not if you hold it for me, dummy!" I yelled back.

Carefully I stepped up in the wagon. Jason went around the pole and grabbed the ladder on both sides. It stopped wriggling.

"Hold on," I urged as I stepped up on the first rung.

Step by step I carefully went up to the top. I hugged that pole with all my might as I stepped on the very top crossbar of that old stepladder. Slowly I stretched my arm up toward the first stake.

"I've got it! I can reach it!" I shouted to Jason. I wrapped my legs around the pole and pulled myself up to the stake. I got one leg over the stake and pulled myself up to the next one. Finally I was able to stand up.

"Come on up, Jason," I called.

"Who's gonna hold the ladder?" he asked.

I laughed. "Guess you gotta do it all alone," I called back down.

While he climbed up the stepladder, I finished climbing to the top of the pole. When I got to the last stake, I looked over at the roof of the morgue. Then I looked down. Suddenly I felt sick. The only thing I'd ever been afraid of was heights, and here I was, way up at the top of a telephone pole.

"Hey, Jimmy, what's the matter?" Jason asked. I looked down again and saw him right below me.

I knew I had to do it. I looked over at the roof again. It was only a couple of feet away.

"Hurry up," Jason urged.

I put both my feet on the same stake and stood there hanging on. I kept my eyes glued to that roof. I let go with one arm and bent my knees; then I jumped! What relief I felt when I hit the roof!

"Yeah, we did it!" I shouted to Jason.

It was his turn to panic. "Nah, I can't make it," he said.

"You oughta see yourself," I teased him. "A chicken sitting on a flagpole. Cluck-cluck-cluck!"

"Move over," he said. "If you can make it, so can I."

He jumped onto the roof. He almost slipped, but I grabbed his shirt and we fell back on our backs. As we lay there a moment, we felt as victorious as Davy Crockett.

"Hey, let's go look inside," I said.

We hurried over to the skylight, but someone had painted all the glass with black paint. We couldn't see a thing. What a disappointment.

"Darn it! I feel like smashing the window in," I muttered.

"Better not. What if they have a burglar alarm?" Jason cautioned. We sat down on the roof, disappointed. Although we'd accomplished most of what we set out to do, we hadn't done it all. But as we looked down at the street below, we started to feel somewhat better. Maybe we hadn't seen any old dead bodies, but we'd won the challenge over that telephone pole; we'd made it to the top.

Soon we found the fire escape on the other side of the building and came down that way, jumping the last ten feet to the ground.

Failure to get something that I wanted was never a feeling that I found it easy to accept. In fact, it always caused me to retaliate if there was any possible way to do so. That desire to get back led to my first skirmish with the law.

During the eighth grade I became a traffic patrol boy at school. We were each assigned a corner to patrol both before and after school. Because I liked bossing the other kids around, I stuck with the job and eventually became one of the patrol lieutenants, overseeing many other patrol boys. I felt really important in that position.

My gym teacher was in charge of the patrols. I had developed a real good positive relationship with him. Because I was so good at all the sports we played, he had spent time with me, coaching me. He was really a great guy, and I liked him a lot.

"You're one of my best lieutenants on the patrol squad," he told me one day, and I glowed with pride.

When one of the two patrol captains left the school, there was an opening for a lieutenant to move up to become a captain. I wanted the job.

"Hey, Mr. Caldwell, make me your captain!" I suggested when I heard about the opening.

"We'll see, Jimmy, we'll see," he answered.

But he didn't give me the job. He moved one of the other lieutenants up to fill the position, which made me furious. And every time I saw the new patrol captain I got angry all over again.

"I'll make him sorry that he snubbed me," I muttered, planning my revenge. I quit the patrol team and refused to speak to Mr. Caldwell. But that wasn't enough. He had let me down; he had failed me. I had to pay him back.

One night I left my house after dark. I didn't tell my mother where I was going, and my dad wasn't home.

I walked over to the school a couple blocks away, carrying that old broken stepladder with me. Carefully I hurried into the alley where the gym door was. I had arranged with a couple of my buddies to meet me there. I had masterminded my revenge, and this was the night to carry out the plan.

"Be quiet," I whispered, "and watch for cars. The police patrol down here at night."

They were scared. I was too, but I sure wasn't going to let them know. Besides, it was up to me to make sure that the plan worked perfectly.

I propped the ladder up in a dark corner and said to one of my buddies, "Okay, you climb up and go in through that window."

I held the ladder while he quickly went up, broke the window, and disappeared inside. We threw the ladder to the other side of the alley and waited by the door. Soon it opened, and in we went.

Quietly and quickly we filled our bags with all the sports equipment we could find. I broke into Mr. Caldwell's office and looted that too. Within ten minutes we'd grabbed all the stuff that we could carry.

Carefully we hurried out the door and down the alley, then ran all the way over to the garage of one of my buddies.

"Yeah, we did it—we ripped off the school!" one of my friends shouted excitedly.

I didn't answer. I just stood there watching them look over all the loot. Somehow I didn't feel as thrilled as they were. I felt tough and big and I could see that teacher's face in my mind.

"Hey, dummies, you wanna get picked up?" I muttered. "Put it all away. We gotta stash it here, not leave it out in the open!" After we hid it all and they went home, I sat there in the dark, just nursing my revenge.

"Ain't *nobody* gonna cross me up!" I thought. "Not without my paying them back." I couldn't wait to see Mr. Caldwell's face when he discovered all his stuff gone. I almost wished I could tell him I had done it.

That's exactly what someone else did. Someone ratted on me, and I got caught. I was suspended from school, and I couldn't go through the eighth-grade graduation ceremony with the other students. I graduated out the back door; someone handed me my diploma across an office desk instead of with a handshake on the platform.

But I didn't care. I'd had my moment of revenge, and it was sweet!

Dad didn't say too much about it. "Oh, Clara, I remember being a boy. At least he graduated," he told Mom, who was bitterly disappointed that I hadn't graduated with all the other kids.

"Aw, Ma, it's no big deal! I got the piece of paper letting me out, didn't I? Who cares *how* I got it?"

"*I* do, Jimmy," she replied. "I don't understand why you do these things. You get in more and more trouble all the time."

I just laughed at her and turned to walk away. She stepped in front of me with a look on her face that made me feel just awful—a look that revealed a blend of hurt, disappointment, and frustration. But I wasn't going to let her know that I cared.

"Someday, Jimmy," she went on, pointing a finger right at me, "someday you're going to be sorry for the things you do!"

I walked out the door.

4. Strike Out . . . Game's Over

My parents' decision to leave Tennessee to move to the big city of Chicago had seemed like a good decision at the time, but now, when I was in my early teens, Dad's dream of success in the big city had turned into the nightmare of bondage to alcohol.

We had come to Chicago mostly for financial reasons. Tenant farming in Tennessee didn't provide Dad with an adequate means of support for our family, and other relatives who had moved to Chicago told him of the possibilities of better money in the city. So they had moved.

But Dad was just a small-town boy from the sticks of Tennessee; although he knew work, he knew no profession. For several years after they moved he struggled with two and three jobs at a time in order to make enough to keep us from starving.

Gradually things began to get better for Dad. He got a good job—one with a future. Because he was a hard worker, a loyal employee, and a fast learner, he advanced in his position. He was highly motivated to achieve, and he had strong leadership abilities—qualities that helped him to become successful in his business. He started making good money, and for the first time in his life he had all the things he had ever wanted.

The glitter of big-city life and the attractiveness of success affected Dad. For awhile we all enjoyed his newfound success.

"Go buy a new dress!" he'd tell Mom, handing her some money.

"How about me? Can I get that bike I want?" I begged.

"Sure," he said. "Let's go get it right now!"

Excited, I climbed in the car. I chattered all the way, describing in great detail how great that shiny new bike was going to be.

Dad laughed. "Sounds like you really want it, son," he said as he pulled to a stop.

I looked out the window. "Hey, Dad, this ain't Maxwell Street," I shouted, worried that he'd changed his mind. Maxwell Street, with its rows of storeowners waiting to haggle with anyone about anything, was where Dad usually took me to buy things. He could bargain the owners down to rock-bottom prices.

"No, son, this time we're shopping right here at Chicago's best sports store," he answered me.

"Wow, let's go!" I shouted, jumping out and running for the door. This was the biggest sports store in Chicago—several floors of expensive, top-of-the-line sports equipment of every kind. I headed straight for the fifth floor, the one with all the shiny new bikes!

Yes, those days were good, but things changed. Dad had always enjoyed a beer at night, but now one or two beers no longer satisfied him. It seemed to me that almost overnight he became a drunk. Life became very different for all of us. I didn't understand it at all.

"Hey, Dad, how about a little catch before my game?" I often asked when he pulled up in front of our house. I was still playing baseball with the Midgets almost every night.

But instead of coaching me on to be a better baseball player, he was usually so drunk that he couldn't even throw the ball back to me. I'd walk away from him in disgust; his baseball playing had become just a farce to me.

Many evenings I'd wait, hoping he'd come home sober, only to discover that he wasn't going to make it home at all before dark. The next morning he'd stumble out of the bedroom full of remorse when he saw my disappointed face. "I'll be there next time, Jimmy—wait and see."

But soon I realized that next time never came. I stopped anticipating playing ball with him. I stopped anticipating *anything* from him.

No longer did I jump in the car, eager to go places with him. When he did take me with him, I ended up wishing I hadn't gone. He often took me to a dimly lit, smoke-filled bar, where he'd shoot pool with all his drinking buddies. I'd sit watching him get drunker and drunker, and with each drink he'd become less and less the hero I'd believed him to be. The anger boiled up inside me.

I felt terrible about Dad's drinking. He was a different individual —an animal—when he drank. He became violently aggressive and abusive to both Mom and me.

One night Dad came home drunk and staggered out to the kitchen, where Mom and I were talking. He opened the refrigerator. Mom guessed that he was looking for something more to drink.

"Don't you think you've had enough, James?" she asked him, stepping over to the door and pushing it shut.

Dad became enraged. Grabbing Mom by the arm, he flung her toward the table. "Hell, Clara, you're not going to stop me from getting a beer," he growled, turning away from her.

Mom began to cry softly. It made me furious to think he'd knock Mom around like that. Without thinking, I grabbed his arm. "Well *I* am, Daddy," I said. "You're not going to knock Mom around like that just to get your beer!"

He grabbed me by the shirt and yanked me closer to him—our faces almost touching.

"You're not man enough to stop me yet, boy," he sneered.

His look repulsed me. "You're a drunken slob!" I said softly.

He raised his arm and slapped me across the face, a blow that threw me back against the refrigerator. He looked at me a moment and then turned away.

My face burned with the rage I held inside. I stood back up on my feet and doubled up my fists with every intention of hitting him back. But Mom grabbed my arm.

"No, Jimmy, just leave him alone!" she implored me.

By that time Dad had staggered into the bathroom next to the kitchen. From where I stood I could see him vomiting all over the floor.

I hate you! I thought as I looked at him. You're not my Dad!

"I gotta get out of here," I told Mom. I walked out the back door, away from that man for whom I now felt so much contempt.

All the trust I'd ever had in him began slowly to crumble into shame and fear. All my memories of happy boyhood years melted away like the ice in his glass of booze. I relived that night many times over, wondering when it would happen again.

Many nights when I came in the house Mom would grab me, saying, "C'mon, Jimmy, hurry! We're going over to Aunt Edith's for supper." I could see the terror in her eyes, and even though she'd try to shield me from the truth, I knew she was simply terrified to be at home when Dad arrived from his rounds at the neighborhood bars.

Those nights when he came home early, he usually came in sick and hurt from fights after work—many times with black eyes, bruises, cuts, the results of violent confrontations with his co-workers.

When he sobered up, he'd cry like a baby about his mistreatment of Mom and me. I got to the point where I expected only two extremes from him—violence or crippling guilt.

Dad and I still went fishing on the weekends occasionally. I never knew what to expect from him on those trips. Sometimes I took along a buddy, knowing that Dad wouldn't be any fun. Jason came along on one of the most memorable of those trips.

"Be right back, son," Dad said as he stopped repeatedly for "just one more beer" as we drove across the city to the Fox River.

"Hey, your dad sure likes to booze it up," Jason said.

"Yah, you ain't seen nothing yet!" I joked, trying to cover up my embarrassment.

Finally we arrived near the fishing spot we'd used a hundred times in the past. As we pulled between the trees, Dad hit one of them, almost knocking all of us into the windshield.

He tried to make a joke: "They must have moved that tree!"

Jason and I spent the night sleeping in the car. Dad spent the night drinking in a nearby bar.

The sun woke Jason and me early. "Hey, c'mon, let's go set the poles up," I said, climbing out of the car.

"Yah, no sense waiting for your dad," he answered.

"Hey, Jimmy, how come you're up already?" I heard Dad call. I looked up the hill to where he stood—hat turned sideways, cigarette dangling, beer splashed all down the front of him, the ever-present quart bottle of beer clutched in his right fist.

He half-staggered, half-fell down the hill to where we sat. "Gotta sleep awhile," he mumbled, falling back on the bank and spilling the rest of his beer all over himself. Embarrassed, I tried to ignore his drunkenness as he fell asleep.

Jason and I fished companionably for awhile, but Dad didn't sleep long. Soon he was ready for more, and he dug out the ice chest loaded down with beer. We watched as he tackled another quart of beer.

Before the day was barely started I wished I'd never come. Dad was bombed out of his head, and it was apparent that he had no intention of doing any fishing. This was simply a drinking trip; he could drink as much as he wanted without Mom to answer to. The only good thing was that he was too drunk to be abusive.

"Help me get him in the car," I said to Jason later that day. We shoved him in the back seat and loaded up the gear, and I jumped in the driver's seat.

"Hey, Jim, *you* can't drive," Jason said with alarm. I was only fourteen.

"Why not? I know how," I muttered. "You want to get home, don't you?"

I drove home across the city, watching in my rear-view mirror all the way for a cop to notice me and stop me. None did, and we arrived home shortly after dark.

I jumped out and started up the steps. Jason followed, saying, "What about your dad?"

Angrily I stopped, glanced at the car, then muttered, "Let the stupid drunk sleep it off!" I'd had all that I could stand.

After that weekend I stopped asking him to play ball with me or to take me places. I quit bringing my friends home with me. In fact, I quit coming home myself! I knew that whether or not he was drinking, he'd only embarrass me with his behavior. I quit counting on him for anything.

I don't need him, I'd think as I saw him staggering home. I don't need anyone; I can take care of myself.

My disappointment in my dad became a key factor in our changing relationship. I found it very hard to deal with my feelings about him. I loved him, but I also hated him, especially when he was drinking. And that was just about all the time.

My sister and her husband were struggling with Dad's drinking also. Jack, my brother-in-law, had been around our family for years. He was short and muscular, an ex-G.I. who wasn't afraid to stand up to anybody. He had fought in World War II and been decorated for bravery. He was a rough-and-tumble kind of guy, coarse in his behavior, but a great big teddy bear inside. He had always been like a big brother to me, and was very protective of my sister, Fran, and of Mom.

One night when he and Fran came over for a visit, Dad was just drunk enough to let down his guard and be his ugly mean self with Mom. He and Jack were sitting at the kitchen table. Dad was drinking beer.

"Get me another one," Dad ordered as Mom walked by. When she didn't comply with his request, he grabbed her arm and pulled her close. "Didn't you hear what I said to you?" he asked.

"Let her go, James," Jack said.

"No one's gonna tell me how to treat my own wife," Dad answered, yanking Mom by the arm until she cowered in front of him.

Jack stood up and said again, "Let her go!"

When Dad refused, Jack grabbed his wrist and pried Dad's hand loose. Jack then helped Mom to her feet.

Just then Dad stood up from the table and started swinging at Jack, staggering toward him. Jack doubled up his right fist and, throwing his weight behind his punch, slugged Dad right in the face. He fell to the floor, out cold.

"Clara, I hated to do it, but someone had to," Jack apologized to Mom. She was too frightened to do much else but cry.

Jack hauled Dad up off the floor and dragged him to the bathroom and into the bathtub, turning the cold-water shower on. Mom, Fran, and I watched from the door.

"It's time I laid the facts on the line to him," Jack told Mom.

When Dad was soaking wet, Jack dragged him out of the tub and across the floor to the front door, leaving a trail of water behind them.

"Jack, it's the middle of winter!" Fran called to him.

"Hell, I don't care. It's time to take care of this problem," Jack answered, dragging Dad soaking wet into the subzero weather. He shoved him into his car and ran around to the driver's side. Rolling down all the windows, he began to drive around.

By the time they came back home, Dad was shivering violently from the exposure. His clothes were frozen stiff, and icicles hung from his hair. Jack helped him into bed, and Mom began to wrap him up in blankets.

"I'm sorry, Clara," Jack tried to explain to Mom. "He made me so mad I couldn't stop myself from teaching him a lesson."

Dad almost died of exposure that night. But from then on he never abused Mom in front of Jack again.

I think that night was the death of our relationship. I had lost all of my respect for this slobbering, drunken shell of a man — a man whom I had idolized a few short years ago. I began to erect a wall of silence between Dad and me. Dad had stopped reaching out to me, and now I stopped reaching out to him.

Not long after that night another change took place in our family. I was fifteen or sixteen at the time, and Dad decided that he had drunk enough. He felt that he was losing his family because of his drinking. He knew that Mom would stick with him, but he couldn't stand the thought of what his drinking had done to me. One morning he woke up sober from the previous night's drunk and called me into the bedroom.

"Son, your dad is going to stop drinking. I'll never drink again." He didn't, either; he simply stopped. But the fact that he had stopped drinking couldn't erase the many disappointments I'd felt during his years of drunkenness.

My dad's decision to stop drinking was not the result of sheer will power alone. He had made a spiritual decision. Years earlier he and Mom had been regular churchgoers, and now he again felt drawn to the church.

That first Sunday after Dad stopped drinking all of us went to church together. What kind of weird church is this? I thought as we sat down in a pew. While we had been standing around outside waiting for the services to start, I had watched the gathering churchgoers as they stood smoking their cigarettes and talking with each other. I heard frequent curses and recognized men from the bar where Dad had taken me to shoot pool. But when the church doors opened, as if on cue their cigarettes dropped and they filed into the pews, sitting there reverently now, looking for all the world like two-faced religious hypocrites.

At the end of a sermon I couldn't understand, the preacher asked, "Is there anyone here today who'd like to come forward to rededicate your life to the Almighty God?"

Mom nudged Dad and said, "Let's go, James." They were both crying as they made their way up to the front. Several church members prayed for them. I thought to myself, It's all a game they play, this church stuff. I didn't believe the change in Dad; I didn't trust him.

In the days and weeks that followed, Dad tried repeatedly to restore the good relationship we'd once shared. But by now the hurt he'd piled on me had built a wall, and I had no intention of tearing it down—and no reason to. I simply didn't need Dad any longer.

"Want to play baseball, Jimmy?" he'd ask when I came home. I'd ignore his question and go into my room, slamming the door behind me. Quickly changing my clothes, I'd walk back out, hurrying to the door to leave again.

"Why are you acting this way, Jimmy?" Dad would ask.

One afternoon I glanced at him and saw the tears welling up in his eyes. All at once I felt as though my heart would break. But I turned away and hurried out the door.

I'd been hurt enough. Besides, I had my own life now. He had quit drinking to save his family, but now I didn't want any part of him.

It broke my Dad's heart—but then, hadn't he broken mine?

5. Strung Out

"Hi, Mike, what's up?" I asked as I opened the door.

"Hey, c'mon," he answered. "I got a friend up on the North Side I want you to meet."

I grabbed my jacket and we ran downstairs to Mike's car.

Sly was sitting in the back seat. Sly and Mike and I had started hanging around together a few months before, and we'd become big buddies, always together. Sly was a husky, sandy-haired, ruddy-faced, big-nosed kid with pimples all over his face. Mike was a short, black-haired Italian guy. They were about as opposite as two guys could be. Sly was ugly, quiet, and mean; the girls stayed far away from him. Mike was a smooth talker, and so good-looking that the gals hung around him all the time. The one thing all three of us had in common was that we were ready for anything, anytime.

"Who's your friend?" I asked as we got in.

"Hey, you're gonna like him," Mike said. "He's got some joints for us tonight."

I'd never smoked pot before. But I never said no to anything.

We pulled up in front of his friend's apartment and walked up the steps. Mike knocked on the door.

"Who is it?" a young female voice called.

"Mike."

The door opened a bit and a slightly disheveled girl peeked out.

"Who are *they*?" a voice asked suspiciously.

"Two of my buddies," Mike answered, "Hey, c'mon, let us in. They're cool!"

We walked into the shabby apartment, sparsely furnished with old, broken-down furniture. The windows were all covered with heavy blankets, and only the bare lightbulb hanging from the ceiling was lit.

There were already several others sitting around in the semidarkness. The air in the apartment was heavy with smoke and smelled like brewing tea.

Someone handed Mike a partially smoked joint. He took a big drag and handed it to me. "Hey, Jimmy, wait'll you try this!" he said with a smile.

I took the joint in my fingers and raised it to my lips. I'd been around a lot of pot smokers and knew just what to do. I took a long drag on it and passed it over to Sly.

"Man, that's good!" I said sincerely. I liked the gentle wave of good feelings that swept over me. I leaned back and waited for Sly to pass it back. I hadn't felt that good in a long time. I wanted more.

That joint was the beginning; from then on I wanted more and more drugs. I'd discovered a new way to blot out the world that I'd found so disappointing. And it was fun! By this time I had turned sixteen and was entitled by law to increased independence. I took it, quitting high school in order to have more time for drugs.

Life at home was getting more and more difficult because of my new lifestyle. "How come you don't play ball anymore, son?" Dad asked one morning. "Any why are you hanging around with Mike and Sly so much? They aren't as nice as some of your old friends."

"Man, they're my best friends! If you don't like them, tough, cuz I do," I shot back. I still felt empty without the closeness Dad and I had shared when I was a kid, but I was determined to put up a good front and never let him know that I hurt. It felt safer to get mad at Dad than to let him get close to me again, so I always seemed to have anger ticking away like a time bomb, then blowing up at the slightest things.

"Wait'll you see what I got tonight!" Mike said one night when I picked him up.

"What is it?"

"Goofballs," he said. "I got us some goofballs."

"All right!" I cheered. We drove down to Lake Michigan and parked. The lakefront was lined with cars, but no one paid any attention to what went on in the other cars. This was a popular gathering spot for fun-lovers of all sorts. We dropped the barbituates. It didn't take long for the pills to get us high—higher than a marijuana joint could get us.

"Hey, I'm going home," I said. "I feel like sleeping it off." So I dropped Mike off and went home to bed.

But Mike wasn't ready to quit. He took his uncle's car and picked up another dopie buddy by the name of Dutch. They hit a tree and smashed the car. Mike was arrested for being high, and Dutch almost died in the accident.

Dropping pills and getting high had become a way of life for us. I liked the feeling of being high. It was a way of avoiding the past—and even the present. I felt as if I were sitting back, calm and relaxed, watching all the emotions I had so much trouble with keep up their frantic pace without me.

And I liked the thrill and excitement of *getting* the pills. I especially liked the reputation my buddies and I were getting in the neighborhood. People knew we were tough, crazy guys. No one messed with us. Other young people with a taste for adventure tried to associate with us, as though we were their leaders, their role models; while the older, experienced addicts let us hang out with them. The attention made me feel important.

It wasn't more than a year from the time I smoked my first joint to the time I moved into harder stuff.

One night I was with another dopie from the neighborhood. "How about moving into the big time?" he asked me with a wink.

"What'cha got?"

"Man, I got a tray of dynamite smack!" he answered.

"Let's do it!" I agreed.

We drove into a gas station down on Jackson Boulevard and went into the restroom. I used my belt to tie my arm off to make the veins pop up, as I'd often seen others do.

He had an outfit for both of us. He tore the end off a dollar bill. "That's it, Jimmy. That's your gee," he told me.

"Stick this jack on the end of the dropper," he went on. I put the needle he handed me on the end of the eye dropper. Then he showed me how to wrap the three-inch piece of dollar bill around the needle and dropper to hold them tight.

"Let's get the fix ready now," he said. He dropped a little of the white powder in a spoon, added a few drops of water, and lit a match under it. As soon as the liquid got warm, the powder dissolved. He dropped a little cotton ball into the liquid.

"There you go, Jimmy. Suck it up with your jack," he told me.

I filled the dropper full of the liquid. Then I found a vein and jabbed the needle in. A little bubble of blood came up the syringe, and I started slowly squeezing on the rubber end of the dropper.

An immediate rush of pleasure exploded in my brain—a tremendous drive like nothing I had ever experienced before. I took off, and I knew I'd never use booze or pills to get high again if I could get more smack. Not even my slurred speech or the dry heaves I had later bothered me.

I didn't consider the consequences of getting involved in the drug culture. We were having *fun*! Sly and Mike and I began using drugs together regularly, and we enjoyed the thrill and excitement of the drug scene. I was living at home, so I didn't have to worry about where I ate and slept. And I was now one of the most popular guys in the neighborhood. We hung out at a restaurant that was owned by an alleged syndicate figure. We had girls hanging around us, and fun when we wanted it. We were able to make things happen.

In between drinking and smoking dope we were joy-popping and dropping pills. We tried anything we could get our hands on: we dropped red devils and yellow jackets and copped heroin and morphine. We stayed high most the time. My parents saw the changes in me, but if they ever suspected I was messing around with drugs, they never confronted me about it.

Chicago was an easy place to obtain drugs. We developed a lot of contacts and connections; the city was loaded with druggists, chemists, doctors, and others willing to supply drugs for the right price.

One night our luck began to change.

I heard a car horn from upstairs. I hadn't really expected anyone, so I stuck my head out the window to see who it was. I didn't recognize the car and began to turn back inside.

"Hey, Jimmy, come on down."

I recognized Walter's voice. I looked again and saw him motioning me outside.

"Hang on, I'll be right down," I called back to him.

I grabbed my jacket and headed for the door. Then I remembered the bag of heroin I'd bought earlier in the day. I reached back in my closet and grabbed my boots. I turned the left one over and caught the bag of powder I'd stashed there. I reached in the right boot and got my outfit. I shoved it all in my pocket and ran down to where Walter was waiting.

"Whose car?" I asked, jumping in the front seat.

"Hey, man, I borrowed it." He winked at me. "Don't worry, we'll drop it off before anyone misses it," he added, seeing my momentary concern.

"Who's worried?" I shot back. "I got us a little party here in my pocket."

We drove down to the Outer Drive and parked along the lake at Belmont Harbor. I split the bag of heroin with him, and we each got our fix ready. It didn't take long until that rush of pleasure hit us. We sat there awhile, nodding out from the effects of the shots.

We were still flying high later when we decided to go for a ride. When we drove by the restaurant that was our usual hangout, a couple of narcs recognized us as dopies from the neighborhood. They must have run a radio check on the car and found out that it was stolen.

"Pull over," we heard.

"Damn," Walter swore as he pulled over to the curb.

"Looks like we're gonna take our party downtown," I said, laughing at the officer. "At least we used the stuff before you got it." I wanted them to know that they didn't scare me.

We both got busted for grand theft. But they couldn't pin a drug charge on us, even though we were high, because we'd gotten rid of all the evidence. It was my first arrest. I had just turned seventeen. The worst part of it was that it happened right before Christmas: I spent my first Christmas away from home sitting in a jail cell.

Mom and Dad were devastated to find out what had happened. Dad had saved several hundred dollars for Christmas gifts. He took that money and got a lawyer for me instead. He couldn't afford to post bail, but after I had spent two or three weeks waiting in jail for a court date, the lawyer got me off.

Dad picked me up. "Why'd you do it, Jimmy? Why'd you do it?" he asked as we drove home.

"Get off my case," I told him. "Walter took the car. I was just riding with him."

"He's no good, Jimmy. Why don't you stay away from those guys? You wanna end up in jail for a long time?"

"Hey, just leave me alone. It'd better than having to listen to you!" I told him.

I could tell that my words hurt him. We rode the rest of the way in silence. Yet I couldn't help thinking about what he'd said. The two- or three-week period in jail had made an impression on me.

I remembered watching the men in jail. Man, are they hard, I thought. They didn't show any kind of weakness—no emotion, no glimpses into how they really felt.

I thought back to how Walter and I had made a joke out of getting busted. I also remembered how scared I'd *really* felt inside. I knew that I wanted to be a success at what I was doing: that is, I wanted to continue to blow my mind with drugs. I remembered what those men in jail had advised me: "Be careful of the mind games on the streets."

On the streets it was the ones who were strong, who didn't let things get to their minds, that led the others. I knew I'd have to be that way to be a success, so I decided to imitate those men, become as emotionless as they appeared to be. I knew the score; I knew that the law of averages would catch up with me and I'd be back in jail eventually. I also knew that the only way to be able to survive either on the streets or back in jail was to become like those men.

"Here we are, son."

Dad's voice brought me back. We were home. I looked fondly through the living-room window. It was January 11, but the Christmas tree was still up, the lights brightly beaming!

I looked at Dad. "She kept it up for you, son," he said.

As I got out, tears burned my cheeks, so I kept my back to Dad. Suddenly I wanted to see Mom more than anything in the whole wide world.

I forced myself to walk upstairs calmly. It felt so good to be home. Then Mom walked out of the kitchen. I almost walked over to her to give her a big hug, but something in her look stopped me.

She pointed a finger at me. "Someday you'll be sorry for the things you're doing, Jimmy!" she said. I saw the tears in her eyes, felt the hurt she felt. But I felt more than *her* hurt. I ached inside to be that boy again who felt my father's arms around me and smelled my mother's homecooked meals as I walked into the warm, homey, and happy kitchen. I felt totally abandoned, rejected, and unwanted by my parents. At that moment all I wanted was for them to love me—but they didn't! At least that's how I felt.

"I'm going out," I told her, walking out the door. Tears ran down my cheeks. "Don't let them show, Jimbo!" I said to myself.

I went down to our favorite restaurant. There I was the hero, Mr. Popular; there I was accepted. I met Sly and Mike and we went out hustling for some drugs. We were in luck: a crooked druggist sold us some morphine.

We went to a gas station on the corner of Narragansett and Belmont. I went into the bathroom planning to shoot the two tablets I had. In my hurry I dropped one of them in the sink. I grabbed for it, but it went on down the drain. I was infuriated. I wanted that morphine. I *needed* that fix. I *craved* it. I couldn't wait until the moment I could hit it.

"I'll never be that short again," I promised myself.

We began doing even more drugs. I made big money buying large quantities of drugs and then selling them for astronomical profits, but I also spent big money feeding my own habit. When times got rough and we didn't have the money we needed for more drugs, we'd hustle harder. Finally the time came when we decided to start mugging people and snatching purses and wallets. Somehow we had to have the money to buy the junk.

We worked out a plan. Another friend, Phil North, had a car, so he became the driver. Walter was going to hold the people while I ripped off their wallets or grabbed their purses. After I said, "I got it!" he would throw them to the ground.

For our first hit we drove to the neighborhood around Damon right off Armitage. It was two or three o'clock in the morning. We parked near an all-night lounge. Eventually a lady came out alone. She was obviously smashed and looked fairly well heeled.

"There's a score!" Walter said. We sat there watching her for a moment. She was middle-aged and slightly heavy. We talked for a moment about whether she was too big and strong for an easy hit but decided we could handle her.

We jumped out of the car. Walter held her and I grabbed her purse, as planned; then Phil drove away.

I heard Walter exclaim, "She's still hanging on!" She had grabbed the fender and *was* hanging on. We dragged her for a number of feet, maybe yards, before she finally let go. I could hear her screaming.

I felt terrible. But neither Phil nor Walter seemed bothered by it at all. I asked, "Did she really hang on?" I looked through the rear window and could see her lying on the ground.

"Yah, she did for awhile," Walter answered.

I laughed, or pretended to. I wanted them to think I was crazy. I couldn't let them see how bad I really felt. But I thought to myself, I wonder if she's dead or alive.

When I got home and lay in bed, I couldn't stop thinking about that lady. As I lay there staring up at the ceiling, I remembered the sound of that scream. How could I do that? I thought; I've never done anything like that to anybody. I couldn't imagine myself mugging someone and then leaving her hurt—or dead. I felt dirty, bad, and guilty. I thought of Mom. What if somebody did that to Mom? The guilt was almost too heavy to bear. I rolled over on my side. "I can't let this get to me—I can't let this bug me," I said aloud. "I'm going to have to do it again."

With that incident I began accumulating guilt that spread over the next thirteen years. But I never let it show. I turned those feelings off and quit thinking about the after-effects of hurting people. I remembered what the men in jail had told me: "Don't let the mind games get to you."

My life become more and more enmeshed in the drug culture. My hours were completely turned around. I'd hustle all night; then I'd cop a fix and get high. I'd sleep it off until two or three in the afternoon, when the cycle would begin all over.

One day I woke up sick to my stomach, heaving and shaking violently. I realized that I had gone beyond the place of choosing whether or not to do drugs again. I craved a fix. Only with a needle jabbing into my veins, pushing narcotics into my bloodstream would I be able to function on that day. Nothing else would be able to stop the heaves, calm the shakes, or enable me to crawl out of that bed. It wasn't a matter of just waking up with a headache and drinking a little booze to feel better, or sleeping it off. I was *addicted*. Even though I was only seventeen, I was a dopie, and it was the pits. I was no longer joy-popping. I was strung-out, hooked, with no apparent way out.

Soon after that, too sick to take care of myself, I was admitted to the psychiatric ward of Cook County Hospital to dry up. A friend drove me, but I went voluntarily. I was too sick to manage my habit, and I thought that a hospital stay would be better than jail. But it was worse—much worse! I was an adolescent, but the experience of that psychiatric ward made me feel like an old, worn-out, helpless bum. Still, I stayed several weeks.

The intake room was bare and cold and white, with three or four chairs on one side. A big metal bathtub stood in the middle of the room.

"Okay, Dycus, strip down and get in the tub," the guard barked at me. I couldn't believe he was serious; there were two or three other patients in the room.

"Get to it!" he ordered again.

When I was done, he threw me a towel and a white gown and pair of pants. Then he took me upstairs to another room—one I soon began calling the snake pit.

Everything I'd ever imagined about a nuthouse came to life before my eyes in this room. Over 100 patients were jammed together in it. There were only a few hard benches in the room, all without backs. I wasn't about to sit on one of them, so I went to the back of the room and slid down on the floor with my back against the wall. I was in such physical agony from withdrawal that I could hardly hold my head up. But when I did, the sight of the other patients repulsed me even more than my own condition. One of them ran by me stark naked, screaming at the top of his lungs.

"God," I cursed, "I hope I'm not stuck here for the rest of my life."

After several days, they moved me to a better ward. But I still hated it. There was only one other addict there among the 200 or more patients—just he and I. We discovered that we were different than the rest. We couldn't have any visitors, and we were never left alone. We were trusted less than even the ones who were so deranged that they didn't know their own names. I couldn't wait to leave—to get back out on the streets where I felt like somebody, felt accepted.

As soon as I hit the streets again I copped a fix. I looked for Mike, but no one knew what had happened to him. He had dropped out, and I never saw him again. Soon after that I got the word that Sly had O.D.'d, dying in a dopie's apartment.

It wasn't fun anymore. Drugs consumed me. I lived to put that needle in my arm, lived to feel that rush. Whatever I had to do to get that fix, I did it. I put all my effort and energy into getting high.

I *had* to stay strung out!

6. Take Me Home

While I was getting more and more involved in the drug culture, my parents were in the midst of their own struggles.

Everything had been going downhill for Dad. While he was still drinking, he lost the supervisory job that he'd held for years. Even after he'd stopped drinking, he was never able to find another good job. The halfway decent ones he did find he soon lost because of a new problem he had developed.

Sometime soon after he had stopped drinking he began hearing voices and seeing things. He lost touch with reality and lived in a world of his own. He could no longer even provide adequately for his family; he was too obsessed with his own mental state.

Mom had a difficult time. They simply couldn't make ends meet. She took in laundry to help, but it wasn't enough. And she tried for months to convince Dad to sell everything they had and move back to Tennessee.

I was too involved in the drug culture to be of any help. Even though I still lived with them, I was never there, never helpful. In fact, I brought them more troubles.

"Hi, Mom," I said, walking in the door one day.

"Jimmy, where have you been? You've been gone for over three days," Mom called from the kitchen. As she came through the living-room door she saw me—and the girl with me—and stopped.

"This is Jill," I said. "We just got married."

"Married!" Mom gasped.

We were both seventeen years old. I'd been dating Jill since I met her—which was all of several months earlier. She was a part of the drug culture I'd become obsessed with. A couple weeks before she'd hit me with the news: "Jim, I'm pregnant. We have to get married."

We drove to Crown Point, Indiana, a popular spot for weddings. In Indiana you could get married under the age of eighteen as long as you had your parents' permission. Forging notes from our parents had been no problem for us.

But there *was* one problem: Jill didn't want her parents to find out that she was pregnant before we got married. We found a crooked official in Crown Point who was willing to move the dates back a few weeks on the marriage license, and we paid him to do just that.

I had no means of supporting a wife, so Jill joined me with my parents. Both of them were opposed to our marriage, but what could they do? We were too young and too messed up to really care about our marriage ourselves. It was only a matter of months until I discovered that there was no pregnancy. I'm not sure if Jill ever really thought there was. That had been the only thing holding us together, so Jill left and we went our separate ways.

Mom and Dad reached the end of hope in Chicago. In 1958, when I was nineteen, they decided to return to Tennessee. They liquidated what little they had, borrowed money to pay off their bills, and moved back home. Mom felt that this move would change things for them financially, because they'd be able to live much more cheaply in Tennessee. She also thought that it would improve my relationship with them. But I stayed in Chicago, close to my drug connections.

By this time I was addicted to heroin and my life was deteriorating rapidly. For several weeks after Mom and Dad left I stayed in their empty apartment with no furniture, electricity, or even running water. When the landlord finally kicked me out for failure to pay rent, I stayed with dopie friends. Getting high was the only thing that made me feel good. I lived to be high. The drugs were taking a tremendous toll on me physically, and I desperately needed help.

One day, in hopes of a free meal, I stopped to see Jack and Fran. I'd been using several kinds of drugs that day. (At this point there wasn't any drug I wouldn't try. I'd even drink nose drops to get high if necessary.) This abuse of drugs had made me desperately sick. I'd lost a great deal of weight and was very weak. I could no longer fight off the effects of my drug habit. I needed to go to the hospital very badly.

"Jimmy, you look terrible. What's wrong?" Fran asked. I was hanging over the sink, my body shaking with dry heaves and convulsions.

"Nothing, I'll be fine," I answered. Wanting to get away from her, I turned to leave the room. I almost passed out but grabbed the kitchen chair to catch myself.

"You're *not* all right! What's wrong?" she persisted.

I knew she was right. I was too messed up to take care of myself and my drug problem alone.

"I'm taking you to the hospital," she told me.

In the car she pressed for answers: "Jimmy, *please* tell me what's wrong with you. I've never seen you look so bad."

"I took something that messed me up," I said.

"What do you mean, you 'took something'?"

Tired of her questions, and too sick to care anymore, I shot back at her, "Drugs, Fran—I took too much smack."

She looked dumbstruck. "Oh, Jimmy, not drugs," she gasped. "Not *you* messed up on drugs."

"Get off my back," I muttered. "Just get me to the hospital."

She was devastated by the news. She knew I'd gotten mixed up with a bad crowd, but she hadn't known about the drugs. She was busy raising her own family, and I avoided spending time with any of my relatives—including Fran. And although she was reluctant to believe that her kid brother was an addict, apparently she never told my parents what was wrong with me. Nor did I: I never even once discussed my drug habit with my parents.

I kicked my habit in the hospital, but I became addicted again immediately after my release. I moved into a dope fiend's apartment on the Near North Side of Chicago. Soon my life was as crazy as it had ever been.

One night I went to a party and got high. I met a girl there, and we decided to have a little fun of our own. But things got rough. She accused me of raping her, and I was picked up by the cops.

I was locked up and spent a week in jail waiting for a court date. Finally the charges were dropped for lack of evidence. But the withdrawal symptoms during that week were horrible, and the guards had no compassion. Worse than the vomiting, convulsions, and aching bones was the depression that set in from my mental anguish. I needed drugs to cover up my guilt; I *wanted* drugs. In fact, the *only* thing I wanted was drugs. I was like a little boy whose favorite toy had been stolen from him. Without drugs I had nothing to stop the guilt from pervading every corner of my mind. And there was no one I could tell about the way I felt. I'd made my choice; I had to be like those men I'd met the first time I was in jail.

I knew that the minute I was released I would be addicted again. I longed for the moment I could make a connection and hit it. And yet a part of me longed to be free of the addiction. I had just enough money for a Greyhound bus ticket to Tennessee. I decided that I would go south the minute I was released, and I did: I stepped right out of jail onto a bus. I didn't even call Mom and Dad to ask if I could come. I just went.

I believed that if I could just get away from my drug sources I could clean up and leave drugs alone. I was scared to death at the realization that my need for drugs was out of control. I felt as though my whole life was up for grabs, and I didn't like how it felt. I was panicked; I knew I had to do something. Otherwise I had absolutely no protection—I was anybody's victim. I *had* to do something! Maybe in Tennessee I can get it back together, I thought as the miles ticked by on that bus.

I got off the bus in Newburn and began the 1,000-yard walk along the railroad tracks to my uncle's house, where my parents were staying.

I've done more to hurt Dad than anyone else, I thought as I walked down the tracks. He's lost his mind because of me. What can I ever say to let him know how sorry I am? I felt so terribly responsible for what had happened to him.

I wondered if he would even allow me to speak to him. My aunts and uncles in Chicago had kicked me out and didn't want me around. Even Fran wouldn't let me in her house when I stayed there—I slept on the porch. She was afraid of me! I wondered how he would feel. I had never before asked my dad to forgive me. It was so difficult, and I couldn't seem to get the words right in my mind.

As I climbed the steep 100-step path up to the house from the tracks, I rehearsed my words, but nothing sounded right. As I stepped onto the front porch, I heard Mom and Dad talking. It felt so long since I'd heard their voices, heard the voice of anyone who really loved me.

I knocked on the door and my mom said, "Come in." I saw Mom first and hugged her. "Where's Dad?" I asked, walking into the next room. And there he was. He looked lovingly at me, opened his arms, and cried, "My son, Jimmy—my son!" I walked into his embrace.

"Dad, forgive me, forgive me!" I managed to say through my tears. His arms around me took me back to my childhood, to the times when I had thrown myself into those arms when he came home from work. I clung to him, shaking with sobs while years of remorse and pain washed away with my tears.

He forgave me instantly. At that moment I felt closer to Dad than I had ever felt in my life.

In those first few weeks in Tennessee I tried desperately to overcome my drug addiction. My parents were hopeful for the first time in years. They didn't really know what I was battling, but they saw my struggle to get my life together. But it was so hard!

One day I was sitting at the window, wanting to be back in Chicago. The old cravings for that needle were terribly strong. I made a fist and looked down at the tracks running up and down my arm. I put my finger on the vein. God, I wish I had a hit, I thought, putting my head down on the windowsill. "I can't do it!" I whispered aloud. Mom came over to me, lifted my chin up with her gentle hand, and said, "You pick up your head, Jimmy!" Her love for and belief in me awoke my hope. She made me feel as though I *could* do it. And I really tried.

Dad and I began to do things together for the first time in many years. After I'd been in Newburn a couple of weeks, he said, "Hey, Jimmy, let's go down to the pool hall and shoot a little pool." I looked at him. I was bored and fidgety and willing to go, but I hesitated. I wasn't sure what state of mind he was in.

"Come on, let's go!" he urged. So we walked the half-mile down the tracks to the town pool hall. For an hour or so we had a great time, bantering back and forth as we challenged each other to game after game. Then Dad seemed to change; his mood darkened suddenly.

"Hey, Dad, it's your turn," I called to him. He was standing by the window, staring out into the street.

"Gotta go," he mumbled. "It's calling me out again. Don't you hear it, Jimmy?"

"Damn it, Dad, there's no voice!" I said, grabbing his arm to pull him away from the window.

Angrily he flung my arm away. "Get out of my way, son. I gotta go!" I followed him out the door, feeling angry and abandoned, jealous of the voice that had taken Dad away from me. I watched him walk away, remembering another pool hall many years ago when I had walked away from him. Now he was walking away from me — again.

For several weeks it seemed that I would be able to make a change. I stayed clean, even left the booze alone. Mom and Dad encouraged me to start playing ball again, so I decided I would. One night I drove to the ballfield in nearby Dyersburg, where one of the best teams in the area was practicing.

"Hi, my name's Jim Dycus," I said to one of the players. "Mind if I play a little ball with you guys?"

"Sure, Yank, come on and play with us," he answered.

From that day on I played shortstop on the team. We had games four or five nights a week. And it was almost professional ball. People came from all over to watch us play. Some of them even wanted to see that Yankee who never missed a ground ball. I had a focus again — something to give myself to, some achievement that made me feel good about myself.

The evening that we won the championship, I felt elated — the crowds in the stands were on their feet cheering — and yet something was missing. I looked over to the stands. I wish Dad were here to see what a good player I've become, I thought. At one time he would have given anything to see me play in a game of this caliber. But now his mind was gone. I knew it was my fault that he wasn't here; I had turned my back on him when I began using drugs. Now it was too late. We couldn't go back.

I walked alone to my car and headed north toward Newburn. On the way I passed a VFW hall. "Hell, it's no use anyway!" I said to nobody, jamming on the brakes. I made a U-turn, pulling into the VFW parking lot. I got out and walked into the bar.

"Give me a double," I told the bartender.

I sat there for hours, drinking glass after glass of booze as memories of the past thundered through my mind. By the time I got up to leave I was stoned. I was in no condition to drive, but I got in my car and headed down the road.

When I came to a place where the highway divides, I saw the lanes leading off to the left and right but couldn't seem to make the decision about which way to go. At the last minute I yanked the wheel sharply to the left. I ran off the road and hit a lamppost, knocking it off its base. It landed on the top of the car and then rolled off to the side. I stepped on the gas and swerved back out on the road.

I looked in my mirror and saw the flashing red lights.

"Damn!" I shouted, "some cop saw me hit that pole." I stepped on the gas again.

The officer chased me about five miles down the road. When I finally stopped he came up and told me to step out of the car. "Do you know that you knocked over a lamppost back there?" he asked.

I could tell by the sarcasm in his voice that he saw my drunkenness.

I saw it too, recognized the caged feeling of being locked to booze and drugs. At that moment I felt the same old bondage flooding back over me that I had tried to escape in Chicago.

"What post?" I asked.

He pointed to the big dent in the roof of my car. "The one that did that," he answered.

Suddenly I laughed. I couldn't *stop* laughing. "Goodbye light, hello darkness!" I laughed some more.

The cop put away his ticket book, grabbed my arm, and motioned me to the squad car. "Come on, buddy, I'm taking you in."

That brief encounter with the law didn't deter my relapse. I just didn't seem to have the inner power needed to change. I began to fall back into my dependence on booze and drugs. I started drinking first. I could keep myself off drugs for short periods of time if I drank enough.

I hung out at the pool hall and at a local inn. Women had always been attracted to me, and I felt good about myself when women were around me. One night I met Caroline, and we started dating. She was young, just out of high school. She was a mama's girl, but fortunately for me I conned her mother into thinking I was all right.

Caroline was a follower and would do whatever I wanted to do. She looked pretty good and danced fairly well. In a small hillbilly town where the pickings were slim, she seemed a good choice. And it was obvious that she wanted to be with me. I was different than the local guys. I was a city guy, street-wise and outgoing. I dressed well; I was very sensitive about my shoes, hair, teeth, and fingernails. A lot of the local guys weren't.

Every night Caroline and I went to the gin mill and drank and danced until I was bombed. Then we'd spend the night in a motel. Somehow she seemed to take away some of my loneliness. But I always seemed to need other women too. I wasn't a one-woman man. I knew that even though I was spending time with other women, using Caroline when I felt like it, still she was there. She hadn't walked away from me.

When I did spend time at home I could see how my behavior was breaking Mom's and Dad's hearts. Many nights when I got ready to go out again, I would find my Dad down on his knees, praying for me.

"Man, don't pray for *me*, Daddy. Pray for yourself," I'd say, laughing as I stepped over him to get outside.

I was getting bombed every day, and it wasn't enough. I began going into the black area of town to get drugs. I'd get different kinds of speed on the streets, or pills or nose drops from the druggist. For awhile I was able to avoid suspicion. But soon I needed more. I loaded myself up with booze and drugs, often stealing money from Dad to buy my drugs.

One night as I was in my parents' bedroom getting ready to leave, I realized that I had no money. But I *needed* some pills. By now Dad had started hiding his wallet from me, stuffing it under the pillow when he went to bed. He was lying on the bed now, watching me get ready, and I could see the disappointment in his eyes.

"Hey, Dad, what'cha doing?" I asked, giving him a gentle punch in the ribs.

"Aw, nothing," he answered.

"Hey, come on, how about a little wrestling match?" I asked, grabbing his leg and pulling on it.

He looked so happy at my signs of apparent affection. We began to wrestle on the bed, and I maneuvered him to where I could get my hand under the pillow. I grabbed his wallet.

"Hold on, Dad, I gotta go to the bathroom!" I said. I left the room, taking his wallet with me. He had only five dollars, but I stuffed the money in my pocket and went back to where he lay on the bed. We wrestled some more—long enough for me to shove the wallet back under his pillow.

"Well, Dad, gotta go!" I said, standing up.

"I wish you'd stay here," he urged.

The next morning when I stumbled into the house Dad was crying. I knew immediately what was wrong. "Jimmy, that was all the money your mom and I had for a whole week," he said to me.

"Hell, I'm not staying here," I mumbled, fleeing the room. I was sick inside at what I had done. But I had *needed* that money.

Soon after that I realized that I couldn't ease my pain with only booze and pills. I wound up in Memphis, where there was a better supply and I could mainline heroin again. Once more I had broken Dad's heart—this time for the last time.

7. The Eye in the Sky

"Jimmy, I want to talk with you about something," Mom said as I walked into the room.

I looked at her more closely, surprised at her greeting.

I'd come back to Newburn for a brief visit from Memphis. I'd arrived the night before but left for a party almost as soon as I arrived home. It was now early the next morning. After a night of booze and drugs at the party, followed by a few hours at a local inn, I was back home.

"Yah, I know, you think I should have stayed home last night," I said. My head hurt, I was coming down from all the junk, and all I wanted to do now was sleep it off. I walked toward the cot they kept in their bedroom for me when I came home.

"Jimmy," Mom called again. Something in her voice made me return to her. I noticed the troubled look on her face as I sat down on the couch.

"It's your dad," Mom said. "He's hearing the voices from outer space all the time now. I'm really worried about him."

I knew about the goofy voices, of course. He'd been hearing them since soon after he stopped drinking back in Chicago. He said that they came from a big eye in the sky. When I came down to Tennessee I knew he was still flaking out on the voices, but I had shoved his problems out of my mind. I had problems of my own.

Now Mom had confronted me with the issue, forced it out in the open. My first thought when I heard her words was one I'd had before: Dad has gone nuts, and it's because of me.

Man, I knew the hurt I'd caused him. Up to now I'd tried to hide from it, but I couldn't do so any longer. Her words exposed my guilt. *I had driven my own father crazy.*

I couldn't help thinking back to all the times I'd hurt him. To the times I'd told him, "Leave me alone, Dad. Let me live my own life." That's what he did to me when he was drinking, and that's what I did to him when I started drugs.

I had stolen money from him, pawned his belongings, even stolen his car repeatedly. I remembered all these things now as I sat there on the couch letting Mom's words sink into my drug-dazed mind.

I thought about one of the last times I'd stolen his car. I had hidden down the street from our house, waiting for him to come home. After he pulled up in front of the house and went in the front door, I pulled a set of keys from my pocket. He'd taken keys from me many times, but each time I had another set waiting. I ran to the car and jumped in. He heard the car start and ran out the front door.

"Get out of that car, Jimmy. I told you never to take it again!" he yelled, running in front of the car, expecting me to stop.

"Damn it, Daddy, get out of my way!" I shouted back. I didn't stop. I swerved madly to the left and barreled away from the curb, not knowing whether I'd hit him or not. Right then, I didn't care.

When I returned home a day or two later, on foot because I'd wrecked the car, Mom was in tears. "Do you know you almost killed your dad?" she asked me. "Someday you're going to be sorry, Jimmy."

"He shouldn't have tried to stop me," I answered. I felt terribly guilty for what I had done, but I never let it show. I pushed the guilt down, trying to ignore it.

But now Mom's words brought it all back up, and I felt the pain again. I glanced at her, sitting there looking at me. "What do you want me to do about it, Mom?" I asked.

"I don't know, son, I just don't know. I don't even know what to do about it myself," she answered, tears in her eyes. I knew she was pleading with me for help; I knew the desperation she felt. But I knew too that I was so messed up I couldn't even deal with my own problems. I had nothing to give!

"Man, I can't deal with this now," I said, walking to the door. "I'm going back to Memphis."

When I moved to Memphis, I had hoped that it could be an oasis in my desert of despair. I couldn't cope with life in Newburn, couldn't handle my need for drugs there. Memphis was a bigger city and drugs were easier to obtain.

Caroline had moved to Memphis also. She had moved in with a friend of hers, and I had stayed with them until I rented my own room from a man who had several rooms to rent. It wasn't long after I moved in that Caroline rented another of his rooms. But while we each had our own rooms there, we stayed in only one of them most of the time.

For several months it seemed as though the move to Memphis had been good. I even got a job working at a large electrical supply store. It didn't pay much, but at least I could pay my rent and buy my drugs.

But I knew that life for Mom and Dad in Newburn was like a time bomb waiting to explode. Every time I called or went to see them, Mom talked about how bad Dad's illness had become. By 1959, before I even left Newburn, he was hopelessly mentally ill. The only way I could deal with the guilt was to shoot enough heroin to obliterate his face from my mind. Mom was left alone to try to deal with his abusive behavior on a daily basis.

I knew how all alone she felt. She had told me one time when I called. She had also said, "Jimmy, I'm afraid your Dad is really going to hurt me." But I couldn't help her; I couldn't even help myself. My drugs were getting completely out of control again.

I began a cycle of drinking and pill-popping to try to handle it. Somehow I managed to hang onto my job, but every night I'd hit the lounges and get drunk. Then I'd get some pills and drop them too.

Caroline and I were living together most of the time, yet I never showed my pain and guilt to her. I just *couldn't* let her see the pain inside. I couldn't risk becoming vulnerable to anyone. So even though I'd take her with me to the lounges and sleep with her at night, we failed to develop any bond, any commitment that let her share my pain. Even after we got married sometime in 1959 and moved into our own apartment, I let her share only my time; she never shared my pain.

During the summer of 1959, Fran and Jack came down to Newburn for a visit. I knew how disappointed they would be in my return to drugs and booze, so I stayed in Memphis. But they drove to Memphis to visit Caroline and me.

Jack confronted me: "Jimmy, how come you've left your mom all alone to try to take care of your dad?"

"I can't deal with Dad anymore!" I shot back angrily.

"Well, maybe it'll help to wake you up if you know just how bad he is," Jack continued. He told me how he and Mom had taken Dad to a psychiatrist to try to get some help. The doctor had diagnosed dad as a paranoid schizophrenic. "The doc said James could become very violent and dangerous," Jack went on. "Is that what you want your mom to have to put up with?" I thought about all the times I'd hurt Dad with my own angry outbursts back in Chicago. I remembered how hard I'd tried to put it all behind me when I came to Tennessee. I even thought about that time I'd asked him to forgive me — and he had. But all I could see in my mind when I thought of Dad was the image of his back as he walked away from me at that pool hall back in Newburn.

"He walked away from me," I said to Jack, "and I'm not walking back to him now."

I went back home to visit only once or twice after that. I spent all my time drinking, trying to forget that image of a dad who walked away from me when I needed him the most.

Years later Aunt Annie told me just how ill Dad had become. His "eye in the sky" had given Dad "instructions" that frightened Mom more than anything else. He'd told Uncle Lester about it one day as they sat talking. "Lester," he said, staring off into space, "God has told me to kill that boy of mine. I'm going to have to do it one of these days."

Mom became fearful not only for her own safety but for mine. She tried to handle him as long as she could. But finally, early in 1960, she couldn't cope any longer. She signed the necessary consent forms to have Dad committed for treatment at the state hospital in Boliver, Tennessee. From that time on she turned more and more to her family for support — especially her father Joe Bridges, her brother Claude, and my Aunt Annie. Many times later she said to Aunt Annie, "That was the hardest thing I've ever had to do!"

Dad never forgave her for that. He spent the last ten years of his life in that mental hospital, but he never believed he should be there. I always believed that I was the one who put him there — and the guilt I felt couldn't be masked with drugs.

8. Folding Chair Failure

"Jimmy, someday you'll be sorry for what you've done!"

Breaking out in a cold sweat, I sat bolt upright in my bed. My head was pounding. I ran my hands across my eyes to wipe away her image.

Since Mom died, I had seen the same image night after night. I saw her finger pointing at me, heard her voice, saw her eyes. Oh, the pain in those eyes.

"Mom," I called, "I'm sorry—God, I'm so sorry! Forgive me, Mom, forgive me!"

The silent room seeemed to echo my words over and over. Forgive me . . . forgive me . . . forgive me. I realized that it was no echo. It was my own anguished voice calling out to an image that by now was gone.

Daylight arrived and wearily I crawled out of bed. Another sleepless night was over. Another hopeless day had begun.

Day after day began the same way. It was as though her death had begun the immediate fulfillment of her words to me: "Someday you'll be sorry Jimmy, someday . . ."

Guilt consumed me, taunted me hour after hour, tortured me until I drank myself into oblivion or dropped enough pills to forget that image momentarily.

Somehow I managed to exist through the morning hours of this day. By the time the afternoon sun had begun to fall behind the hill outside the window, I felt like a caged animal.

"I gotta get out of here before I go mad!" I said to myself, grabbing my shotgun and running out the door.

I walked over to the cornfield behind my uncle's house. Aimlessly I wandered down the rows of dried-out cornstalks. I kicked one over, thinking as I did so that I had become like that stalk—dry and parched on the outside, dead inside.

I aimed my gun and shot at a jackrabbit as it ran away. I'm glad I missed you, rabbit, I thought. Nobody should have to die.

So why did *she* have to die?

Just then the afternoon train went by on those same tracks. I couldn't bear to hear it, yet I couldn't stop the awful rhythm of its wheels calling out to me: "You'll be sorry, you'll be sorry . . . sorry . . . sorry . . . sorry!"

In desperation I wheeled around and shot again. The echo of my shot pierced the quiet afternoon stillness.

Nighttime fell, and I knew it was time. Time for what had become a daily ritual. I crossed the yard to the porch, dropped the shotgun, and picked up the folding chair.

I turned around and looked blankly across the front yard, across the street to the cemetery on the other side. I took a step, and as I did so I subconsciously started counting. I knew that by the time I reached 100 I would be standing in front of her grave.

I set up the chair and sank into it. For a moment I sat silently, just looking at her name: Clara Dycus. Then my eyes fell down to the dates below: Born, March 27, 1903. *Died*, July 18, 1961.

The dam broke within me. Sobs wracked my body and I cried out over and over, "Mom, forgive me. Mom, forgive me!"

But her grave could offer no forgiveness. Instead, I heard her voice again: "Jimmy, someday you'll be sorry for what you've done!" I saw her finger pointing at me, saw her eyes filled with pain. I reached out to embrace that image and fell into the grass beneath her headstone.

Night after night I thought about the agony Mom had endured during the last six months of her life. After admitting Dad to the state hospital in Boliver, she had returned to Newburn. I can't recall many of the events of those six months, but they must have been sheer hell for her.

Dad hated her for committing him to the mental hospital. Yet every two weeks she would travel the sixty miles to visit him. Because of his frequent violent outbreaks, Dad was subjected to shock treatments that left him in a catatonic stupor. Because of these treatments, combined with the scheduled drug therapy he was receiving, he would rarely function above a silent retreat into his own private world of imagined horrors. Yet many times the very sight of Mom when she appeared was enough to drive him into a violent, crazed verbal assault against her.

Each time she went, she came back home a little more depressed and broken. Putting Dad in that hospital had been the hardest thing she ever had to do in her entire life. It left her so alone!

"Come home, Jimmy, and go with me to see your Dad," she pleaded with me regularly on the telephone.

"Oh, I don't know, Mom. Not this week — I can't come this week," I almost always answered her.

I was still living in Memphis with Caroline, wrapped up in my own private misery, hopelessly addicted to heroin again. Drugs and alcohol had made my life a nightmare. I was getting bombed on booze every night, trying to avoid my need for drugs. But then I'd go and get the drugs and use them too. I couldn't live without that high, that rush of heroin racing through my veins. That was all I cared about. I didn't have the capacity to care about anyone else. Not about Caroline. I was isolating myself from her so that she wouldn't know I'd lost control, wouldn't see the despair I felt inside. Not about Dad, rotting away in that mental hospital. Not even about Mom, living her broken life all alone in Newburn.

"Jimmy, why don't you care about your dad?" she'd ask me. She didn't know how messed up on drugs I was; she never knew that! She only knew that now, in her darkest hour, her little Jimmy didn't seem to care.

When I did go back, did drive her down to visit Dad, it would be so awful that I couldn't stand it.

"Jimmy, is that you, son?" Dad asked one day as I walked into his room. "How about a little catch, son?"

Then he grabbed my arm, his face terror-stricken. "There it is, Jimmy. It's looking right at me, coming right for me!" he screamed, pointing at his imaginary eye in the sky. God, I hated hearing him talk about that!

Mom heard him screaming and rushed into the room. When he saw her, he changed immediately. The terror was gone. Instead, he became violently enraged, and lunged at her, yelling at the top of his voice, "I'll get you. I'll kill you for putting me here. I hate you, woman, do you hear me? I *hate* you!"

I grabbed Mom and pushed her out of the door. By now the orderlies had come and struggled Dad down on the floor, where they were tying on restraints.

"*She* did it, Jimmy. *She* did it!" he called to me as I ran out the door. I joined Mom, who was crumpled in a heap on the bench outside the door, her small body shaking with sobs.

"Let's get out of here," I mumbled. We drove the sixty miles back to Newburn in silence. I dropped her off and immediately drove back to Memphis.

Gotta get a fix, I thought all the way back. That's the only way I can forget.

Yet Mom coped with her private hell alone. She tried to keep some evidence of normal life around to counteract that hell. That's what she was doing on the morning of July 18, 1961. Jack and others have helped me reconstruct that last day.

Mom was canning some tomato relish to give to Jack and Fran when they came down from Chicago for a visit. She needed more lids and decided to walk into town to get them.

It was only a short half-mile walk down the railroad tracks to town. She'd made that walk many times before.

She went down the hill to the tracks and started walking. The afternoon train was due. It always came on the left tracks. This time, however, it approached on the right tracks, the ones on which Mom was walking. The whistle blew; she kept walking. The cow catcher hit her in the head, and she died instantly.

Fran and Jack got the news in Chicago and came immediately.

My cousin called me in Memphis. She reached me at the store where I worked. "Your mom was killed this morning, Jimmy," Gracie said. I dropped the phone, numb from the news. When I reached for the phone again, I somehow expected to hear Mom's voice on the other end.

It was dead — the phone was dead, like Mom! I threw it down, sank into a chair, and covered my face with my hands. Suddenly I heard her voice. "Jimmy," she called.

"Is that you, Mom?" I asked. She called again. Then, "Jimmy, someday you'll be sorry!"

I grabbed the telephone receiver lying by my feet and yanked the cord out of the wall. *Still* I heard her voice calling softly, "Jimmy, Jimmy . . ."

I couldn't stand the pain her voice brought to me. I stumbled out to my car and reached under the dash where I hid my outfit. I needed that fix!

Caroline and I came from Memphis and met Fran and Jack at the funeral home. I'd fortified myself with drugs. I remember standing there talking to the funeral director. I didn't really feel anything once the drugs took hold — until they let us see Mom for the first time.

"Someday, Jimmy, you'll be sorry!"

In panic I fled the funeral home. I hadn't seen her lying there in the casket. I had seen her—I saw her still—standing before me with her accusing eyes, her pointing finger, saying, "Someday, Jimmy, someday you'll be sorry!"

God, was I sorry! I put my hands over my ears, trying to shut out the sound of those agonizing words that kept repeating themselves over and over. "Mom, forgive me," I cried in anguish.

Suddenly a fear gripped me, boiling up within until it pushed its way out through my thoughts. How could this thing have happened? How could a train have hit her? I'd walked those tracks 100 times with her, and she'd walked them many times alone. There's just no way a train could have taken her by surprise and struck her.

By now I was shaking with the fearful thought. What if she—I couldn't get the whole thought out.

Fran, who had walked outside to get me, was shaking my shoulder. "Jimmy, why don't you answer me?" she cried. Mom's death had devastated her.

"I didn't hear you," I mumbled back.

"She's not right, Jimmy. She doesn't have her glasses on!"

We checked with the funeral director, who said there had been no glasses with her.

"Mom never went *anywhere* without them," Fran said.

I glanced behind the funeral home to where the railroad tracks ran. "Let's go find them!" I had to make it right.

We began our walk back down the tracks. With each step I took I heard her voice again. "Sorry . . . sorry . . . sorry!" We approached the spot where they had found her, and the pain was so intense that I had to step off the tracks. As I stepped into the bushes by the side of the tracks, I saw her glasses and I reached to pick them up. Suddenly I saw her face again: "Somday, Jimmy, you'll be sorry!"

I crumbled to the ground. Again the fear pushed up the thought, What if it *wasn't* an accident?

Just then the old man who lived at the top of the hill beside the tracks came down to where we were standing. "Sorry about your mom, miss," he said to Fran. "I saw it happen."

Fran didn't answer; she was overcome by her emotions.

The old man turned to me. Not really knowing what to say, he muttered, "Yep, I saw it all. She didn't suffer, son—she died instantly."

I looked from him to the tracks. For an instant I heard the whistle, felt the throbbing of the tracks, heard the sound of her bones breaking on those tracks.

The old man's hand on my shoulder brought me back.

"Yep, I'm sorry, son," he said, then turned to go back up the path. Then he stopped, shook his head, and turned back to face us.

"I just can't understand it," he said to no one in particular. "It looked to me like she stepped right in front of that train!"

There it was—the fear—only this time all the doubt was gone. I *knew*!

The rest of that weekend was a nightmare. Dad was brought to the funeral home. He walked up to Mom and stood looking at her with his hands in his pockets, a cigarette dangling from his lips. Not a single emotion registered on his face. He turned his back, sat down in a corner, and remained there all weekend. It was as though he didn't feel a thing.

On Sunday afternoon I walked out and over to my car. I drove the half-mile to my parents' house, now filled with relatives. "Gotta wash my car," I mumbled to an aunt. I grabbed some rags and a pail and went back out. I saw their faces, read their thoughts: This just proves that he didn't care about her. He doesn't feel a thing!

I went on scrubbing that old junker car. Gotta get it clean, I thought. Gotta make it right.

Just then I heard the whistle from the afternoon train.

There she was again. I saw her standing there, finger pointing: "Someday, Jimmy, you'll be sorry!"

"Forgive me, Mom, forgive me!" I scrubbed even harder. Suddenly I knew that I couldn't talk my way out of it any longer. I'd lost all opportunity of ever asking her to forgive me. She'd never see me change my ways. I'd *never* make it right! It'd never be clean again! The truth hit home: *she stepped in front of that train because of me!*

After the funeral I had to find out more. Fran wrote to the train company and somehow got the name and address of the engineer, who lived in Memphis.

I took Dad with me. I planned to drive him back to the hospital later that day. Though I was afraid of what the engineer would tell us, I had to know the truth. He invited us in, sat us down on his couch. His wife stood beside his chair. He didn't want to talk about it. I could tell he was still shaken by what happened. But I *had* to know.

"Man, just tell me how it happened," I pressed him.

He was visibly upset. "It wasn't my fault," he cried out. "I blew and blew the whistle, but she just stayed right there! I didn't do it."

There it was—the truth again! His words were like a ton of bricks hitting my chest. But it wasn't just the sudden impact of the words. The weight of guilt continued to press on me. It seemed as though the weight was paralyzing me; I couldn't move.

I glanced over at Dad, who seemed to have absolutely no reaction. "Damn you, Daddy," I thought. "You don't even care!"

But *I* did! Somehow I had to get out of there. I looked at the engineer. He felt my pain—I could see it in his eyes. I had to leave. I grabbed Dad by the arm and we walked out to the car.

No one else suspected the truth—ever. But I knew. The worst part was that I knew and couldn't tell anyone. I couldn't have taken it if people knew, and blamed me. But to me Mom's death was an immediate fulfillment of her words: "Someday, Jimmy, you'll be sorry for all you've done!"

Caroline and I returned to Newburn, to my parents' house. That night I made my first walk to her grave with my folding chair.

I took that tortured journey many times in the next few months. We didn't return to Memphis right away. I had to be close to Mom. But nothing could erase the pain. Even the drunken stupors and stoned trips on drugs seemed only to accelerate my agony. Finally I fled back to Memphis with Caroline. When we got back, I felt driven by the load of guilt. I hit the lounges more than ever, and I began running around with other women. It seemed as if I was trying to fill that mother-void with them. But it was all so meaningless to me.

My drinking got much worse. I couldn't pay the bills, and I lost my job. On top of all my agony, Caroline hit me with some more news—news that I didn't want to hear. "I'm pregnant, Jim."

"Man, that's all I need right now," I said. I was simply incapable of shouldering responsibility for another human being. I couldn't even manage my own life. I was so wrapped up in my own self-hatred caused by guilt that I couldn't care for anyone else. I couldn't "love my neighbor as myself." All I felt was hatred.

Caroline moved back with her parents, and I moved back to Newburn to live with an uncle. I didn't feel that bad about blowing it with her. I didn't even think about the fact that I would soon become a father. I was cut off, alienated from life itself. Sin had claimed my soul. I saw my son Scott only once or twice after his birth in May of 1962.

Nothing mattered anymore—nothing but the horror of that 100-step journey into pain every night. I decided to leave Tennessee and return to the familiar drug culture of Chicago. Maybe there I could forget!

On Thanksgiving in 1961 I went to visit Dad. I knew that this would probably be the last time I'd see him in a long time. I picked him up at the hospital and we drove to my uncle's house for dinner. Dad was so enmeshed in his mental derangement, and I was so consumed by my drug addiction, that that special closeness we had once felt was like a broken dream between us. In its place was just an empty preoccupation with our individual problems.

I sat in my car that evening and watched as the attendant led him back into the hospital.

I'm so sorry, Daddy, I'm so sorry, I thought. I'm *so* sorry for how I hurt Mom and you!

My life was in a shambles. I simply couldn't deal with the guilt any longer. I grabbed the wheel so tightly that my knuckles turned white. I couldn't stand the pain. "I gotta get out of here!" I screamed, heading out the driveway and down the road.

I drove for thirty minutes or more before I realized that I was headed back for Newburn.

"No!" I screamed, "I *can't* go back to Newburn." I yanked the wheel and drove off the road into the ditch. I sat there, absorbed in my pain.

Gotta get out of here, gotta get back to Chicago, I thought. *Gotta have a fix!*

I reached under the seat and felt for the plastic bag that I had stashed there with my outfit. I pulled it out and began to roll up my sleeve.

9. Monkey on My Back

When Fran and Jack came down for a visit with Dad, I rode back to Chicago with them. I'd hocked my car for drugs. As we drove past the towering skyscrapers of the downtown Loop, I knew I was home, back where I belonged. My mind raced with the anticipation of making a connection, getting a fix, finding a chemical means of forgetting the horrors that my memories of Tennessee had bound me to.

"You can stay with us awhile, Jimmy," Jack told me.

Even though returning to Chicago had intensified my desire for drugs, I tried to stay clean. I got a laborer's job and saved a little money. I decided to send for Caroline and my baby son, to try and live a normal life. I rented a small apartment in preparation.

"I've got us a place to live, and I even bought some bedroom furniture," I told her on the phone. "I'll send you a bus ticket and you can come up here with me."

"No, I'm not coming," she replied firmly. She had decided that I was too big a risk, and I didn't blame her. We never saw each other after that. She took me to court for child support, which I agreed to pay but never did. I moved away from Fran and Jack's house, into the apartment that was to have housed my family, and the cops never found me to haul me back to court. A couple of payoffs from a friend satisfied them, and they quit looking for me. I didn't see my son again for more than twenty years.

I met a guy at work who liked to party as much as I did, and we began to make the Rush Street nightlife scene. I was spending all the money I could earn on booze and clothes, building an image of success. I was still avoiding my desire for hard drugs, satisfying my cravings and dulling my memories with pills and booze.

At work I met Jan. We began to date and within a few months we married. She had a job and an apartment; she fit my image of a normal life. But I didn't try to live a normal life. I continued to make the rounds at night. Sometimes Jan went with me, but even if she didn't, I still went. There were always other women willing to party with me. Many times I'd get bombed and shack up with a woman in a motel. Then, when I woke up in the middle of the next day, I'd go prancing home to Jan. She put up with that from me. I've never known why she put up with so much for so long. I wasn't worth it, but she loved me. Maybe she saw something in me that I couldn't see, or be.

I needed to supplement my income in order to live the lifestyle I had created for myself, so I began to hustle pool. I had learned to shoot pool back in Tennessee from a fellow who was supergood. I was very good at the game too—and very good at gambling with it. Not too many people could beat me, but a lot would try.

At the pool hall I met a bunch of boozers who played golf as well as pool. Some of them had a job with a consumer products company, but they never really worked. They cheated on expense accounts, falsified reports, and lived high off the profits. If I could ever get a job like that, I'd have it made! I thought.

I began playing golf regularly with them. It was another way to hustle up a little extra money, and I got to know these guys a lot better. We played golf during the day and partied all night.

I lost my job, but I didn't care because my friends had helped me get the job I really wanted with the consumer products company.

I became a factory representative for the company. I was salaried, so the money was always there. My job was to visit stores, check on the merchandise, and make sure everything was fresh and in good order. All I had to do was falsify my reports and say I'd been in the stores. Then my time was my own. My supervisor did the same thing, so he was no threat to me.

Now I had it made. I'd found a way to support my lifestyle, buy my booze and pills, and build my image as a high-rolling party man.

Jan no longer fit my image. She didn't like my life, hated my friends, and despised my new job. By now she was seven or eight months pregnant, and I couldn't see a future for us.

We decided to change apartments soon after I got the new job. "My uncle's got a place we can rent above his house," Jan told me.

"Okay, get it," I agreed. She packed our things and planned the move. Being pregnant, she was glad to be moving closer to her family. My lifestyle had taken its toll on her. She never indicated that she knew how I was living, and I never told her anything about what I did when I was gone. I don't know if she knew about the other women, but she certainly knew that I was never with her. Somehow she felt that this move would help us both, get us ready for the birth of our first child. But I had different plans.

The day came when it was time to move to the new apartment.

"I got a truck," I told Jan. "We'll take the stuff over tonight after work."

That night a couple of guys from work helped me load up the truck with most of our belongings. We took it over to her uncle's house and set it up in the little attic apartment she had rented.

"Thanks, guys, I can get the rest," I told them when we had almost finished.

I looked around the little apartment, looked over to where Jan stood, big with child.

I felt bad about what I was about to do. I knew that my decision would devastate her, and I tried not to think about what it might do to my unborn child. I still felt terribly guilty about having deserted my son back in Tennessee. But I knew the bondage that drugs held me in. I rationalized that Jan and Caroline and my children were really better off without me. I had no choice: I couldn't live without my drugs. I also chose for Jan: she didn't need a bum like me.

"I'll go get the rest," I told her. "You stay here and start unpacking."

I walked out the door, never to return again. I deserted Jan that night. I'd become a user of people, just as I was a user of drugs. Jan was all used up. I didn't need her any longer.

I didn't see her again for several months, maybe a year. Then I got a summons to appear in court for the divorce hearing. Apparently she traced me through my job. I can still remember the look of hate in her eyes when she saw me. We have a son whom I've never met.

About that time I started losing control of my drugs again. The partying and boozing had camouflaged my drug habit for awhile, but they could no longer do it. The memories of my parents, along with the fresh memory of what I'd done to Jan, to that little son I'd never seen, took more than booze and pills to obliterate from my mind.

My chemical dependence on drugs became a monkey on my back that demanded all my attention. I planned my life around satisfying my cravings. I developed a cycle of drug use that satisfied my needs while allowing me to stay halfway straight.

For a period of weeks or months I drank all the time, night and day. I thought that the excessive use of booze would allow me to avoid the use of hard drugs and would be my salvation from getting too strung out. Soon the booze was not enough, however. I switched from booze to pills, or tried pills and pot along with booze. This combination worked only for a short time too. Then I started mainlining again, shooting drugs to meet my needs. When I got too strung out to keep control, I switched back to the booze, starting the cycle over again. All the while I continued living the fast life, hitting all the lounges along Michigan Avenue.

My job with the consumer products company let me live the way I wanted. I was bringing in enormous amounts of money by deception and false reporting. Because I never had to work, I had the time to hustle golf and pool. I was able to forge prescriptions to obtain my drugs, and I wrote checks or sold drugs to cover the cost of the drugs. Women still seemed to be attracted to me, and I saw that I had the knack of being able to use them to serve my own purposes. I felt I had it made. It was during this time of my life that I met Connie.

I had spent the afternoon playing golf with a couple of friends from work. I had picked up quite a lot of money from the bets, so I was in a good mood.

"Hey, let's party tonight," Zack said as we walked to our cars.

"Let's start now," I encouraged. I reached under the spare tire in the trunk and pulled out a little bag of pills — a crazy assortment of yellow jackets, red devils, and psychedelics. We all grabbed a few and headed for the bar in the clubhouse. We spent a couple of hours there, and then they headed home.

I met a couple of my dopie friends and headed down to one of the lounges on Michigan Avenue. I was high from all the pills and booze, and it wasn't long until we dominated the scene in the lounge. I loved the attention we were getting.

"Hey, c'mon beautiful, let's dance," I said, pulling one of the girls sitting at the bar onto the dance floor. We circled the floor, putting on a show for the whole place — except for one table toward the rear.

Six or eight people were sitting around that table, laughing and drinking. One of the girls seemed to be the life of the party. She was one of the most beautiful girls I had ever seen. I still remember what she was wearing — a powder-blue sweater with a skirt — and she had long black hair. I caught her eye and smiled at her. I knew that she saw me, but she turned back to her friends, ignoring me. I was intrigued and challenged. I sat on the stool watching her for awhile. I could tell that she was high herself, and yet she managed to remain the pivot of conversation at her table. Everyone there was eating out of her hand.

She's good, I thought. She lights up the place.

I turned back to the party my friends and I had going in the rest of the lounge, but I kept my eye on the girl in the back.

A little later she wandered up toward the front to the ladies' room. On her way back to her table I stopped her. "Hello," I said. "Looks like a nice little party you've got going in the back."

"It is," she said, smiling at me. She watched me a minute, then turned to walk away.

"Hold on a second," I said, holding her arm. "How about a dance with me first?"

"Why not?" she answered.

I learned that her name was Connie. She appeared to be a very confident, smart, independent person, and that attracted me. As we sat at a table talking after our dance, she explained that she didn't care for weak people. I liked that. By the time the night was over, I knew that I wanted to see her more—lots more!

We began to date and spent most of our time partying. She knew that I was into something but assumed it was some lightweight drugs. I would still smoke pot or occasionally drop some pills, but most of the time alcohol kept me flying. Connie was divorced and had had a bad time of it. There were hurts near the surface that were always threatening to break through. Partying seemed to deaden the pain a little.

We both liked the fast life. I had to be creative with her, and I enjoyed the challenge of being with her, hanging onto her. We soon began living together. I cared a lot for her, and she probably handled me better than any person I had met until that time.

Early in 1965 my divorce from Jan came through, and Connie and I immediately got married. It seemed as though I had finally made it. I liked my life and at twenty-six had the things I thought I needed to be a success. My drugs were manageable at last, and I could get them any time I wanted them. I had a terrific job and plenty of money. I could golf and play pool whenever I wanted. I even began to bowl, and soon discovered that that was another great way to win a few extra bucks. I had a beautiful wife who liked to party as much as I did.

The job at the consumer products company had become very important to me. I had manipulated my way up to become a field representative for the best area, the downtown Loop area. I came in contact with a lot of successful people and spent a lot of time drinking and socializing in the better lounges. It was at this point of my life that I recognized another profitable source of income.

I had known for some time that women were attracted to me, and I had learned to use them to serve my own purposes. I also knew that there were a lot of successful businessmen looking for a girl on the side. My job provided an excellent cover for me to work this knowledge into a profitable business arrangement. I started hustling women the way I had learned to hustle drugs, golf, pool, and bowling. In short, I became a pimp.

Connie didn't know what I was doing. She saw the guys I hung around with at work, but she didn't see the second set of acquaintances that I had. It would be some time before she suspected anything. Nor did anyone else know about my additional business career. I was very careful to conceal my involvement with women.

The more involved I became with this new business, the more I liked it. It fit the image I was building for myself. I enjoyed the attention from the women and the reputation I'd earned among the men. And the income enabled me to become even more heavily involved with drugs. I started shooting up more and more. I didn't see it then, but this monkey on my back was pushing me closer and closer to the brink of destruction.

10. Destined for Destruction

As I grew more and more dependent on chemical means of blotting out the pain in my life, Connie's life had become more and more secure. I had become very adept at hiding my extracurricular activities from her. She knew only the people I wanted her to know. I did only the drugs I wanted her to know I did. I hid the rest.

Our marriage had been good for her. Her insecurities had been met, and she changed. Gradually she eased out of life in the fast lane. She didn't need the excitement of living on the edge any longer. The partying we had done earlier were her attempts to cover her hurts. She'd had a rough time through her divorce. She was also an orphan and had always felt the rejection of her real parents. Even her adoptive parents had been unable to change that. But our marriage had. When I asked her why she didn't want to hit the lounges with me anymore, she said that she didn't need the kicks, that I was fulfilling her needs. Her values, her morals were changing for the better. Life was no longer a cabaret for her.

Her adoptive parents lived on the South Side of Chicago. She hadn't spent much time with them in a long time. Now she wanted to.

"Mom and Dad want us to come spend Sunday with them, sweetheart. Can we go?" she asked me.

"Nah, let's go out with our own friends. We don't need a bunch of family checking us out," I answered.

"Oh, please, let's go see them," she begged. She had a form of control over me that no one else had ever had. Because I wanted to please her, make her happy, I found it hard to resist her requests.

"All right, if that's what you want," I agreed.

So we went. Again and again. We began spending many Sundays with them for dinner. She had a big family—aunts and uncles and cousins all over Chicago—and most of them seemed to come each Sunday. It reminded me of old times back in Tennessee with my family. The memories were tough on me, and I resented going for that reason. But we went.

Many times I'd sit and drink all day with her brother while Connie visited with the rest of her family.

One Sunday a couple who were friends of her brother were also invited to the family dinner. The wife was a really good-looking chick. By late afternoon that day I was bombed. She and I had been throwing passes at each other all afternoon. Now she stood by my chair, arm over my shoulders. I was enjoying the attention.

"Hey, how about going for a little walk with me?" I asked her, standing to put my arm around her.

"Sure, honey, let's go!" she answered me, and we walked out the back door.

Her husband had been eyeing us since the flirtation began. He was standing out in the back yard as we walked out, ready to make a grab for me. As he lunged at me, I grabbed his head and led his moving body right in the direction of the bumper of a car parked nearby. He hit the bumper and fell to the ground. I laughed as he lay there motionless.

Connie heard the commotion and came running out. Seeing what had happened, she grabbed me by my arm and pushed me into our car and drove us home. While I ranted and raved about the guy I'd just decked, she listened calmly, soothing my anger until it was gone.

"Jim, why do you drink so much?" she asked when I was quiet.

She really didn't know, of course. She didn't know why Mom had jumped in front of that train. She didn't realize that Dad was rotting away in a mental institution right at that very moment because of me. She hadn't seen the times I'd sat and brooded about the two little sons I'd cast away but couldn't forget.

I didn't open up my wounds to anyone. I'd learned to isolate my hurt deep within, where no one saw it. It was eating me alive, but the walls of self-protection were so thick that I couldn't let even Connie's love for me penetrate to where I hurt. But the hurt inside was like a fermenting volcano—looking for a place to erupt!

"Why don't you slow your pace down a little, Jim?" Connie asked me now.

"Why should I?" I shot back. "If you want to sit home, do it, but leave me alone. "I like my life the way it is!"

Instead of turning away as I expected her to, she walked over and put her arms around me. "I like my life too, sweetheart," she told me. "I like our life together, and I want it to go on. Especially now."

"What do you mean, 'especially now'?" I asked.

"Especially now that we're going to have our first baby," she answered with a smile.

When Katie was born in 1966, Connie quit working and stayed home with the baby. Katie fulfilled her needs even more than I did, and she had no desire for the fast life any longer. I tried to slow down too. I even tried to get my drug needs back under better control—at least in front of Connie! Because she assumed I was working during the day, I'd drink then, get wiped out. Then I'd take some pills and sleep it off.

But I wasn't successful at hiding my problem from her for long. By the time Katie was a year or so old, my dependence on drugs was completely out of control again. I went back to the old cycle of using booze to keep me off the hard stuff. And it took a lot of booze to do that.

Many times I sat home all day drinking a fifth of whiskey, no longer pretending to go to work. Katie was old enough to walk around by this time. One day she walked over to the coffee table with her little cup. She grabbed my bottle and began to try to pour some whiskey for herself.

"Jim, stop her!" I heard Connie call. She ran over to the table and grabbed the bottle out of Katie's hands.

"Jim, do you see what she's doing?" she accused me.

The whiskey in me made me start to laugh, but the look in Connie's eyes quickly stopped my laughter. She picked up Katie and left the room.

Man, what am I doing? I thought. What am I doing to Connie and Katie? I detested the person I had become. I felt terrible about the animal I was becoming. But I couldn't change!

I threw the bottle across the room and walked out into the night. I needed a fix!

As I used more and more hard drugs, my need for money grew. My drug habit was costing me anywhere from $100 to $300 a day! Even falsifying reports at work couldn't bring in *that* much. And hustling golf and pool would buy me drinks, but it couldn't keep me supplied with drugs. I concentrated all my efforts at increasing my income with my other business—hustling women.

I worked out a sophisticated business arrangement with the girls. I never *forced* them to work for me. I manipulated them in other ways:

I helped them raise their standard of living, attract a better clientele; I introduced them to drugs and got them dependent on me for their drugs.

They weren't the ordinary, run-of-the-mill prostitutes from the street. They were sharp, attractive, appointment-only girls. Consequently, while there were fewer tricks they turned, they were better, and the money was good. I split the profits half-and-half with them.

Some of the girls had legitimate jobs as secretaries. I liked that, because it gave them a cover. I knew I couldn't risk getting busted, so I did everything I could to hide this business venture. No one really knew the part I played in all of it.

I began by fixing up my business acquaintances, who knew I always had a lot of women around.

One day my boss took me to lunch.

"Hey, Jim, do you know a good-looking woman?" he asked me.

"Yes, I know a number of them. What would you like?" I answered.

He listed his requirements: young, good-looking, and exciting.

"Well, I can fix you up with that," I told him.

"How much?"

"I'll take care of that!" I wanted to make sure that our relationship was good. I wanted something on him so that even if he caught me cheating on monies, or falsifying reports, I'd have some leverage with him.

We made an appointment and I told him to meet me in the parking lot of a motel on Lincoln Avenue near our offices. I picked up Nora, a good-looking, well-built girl in her early twenties. As I introduced them in the parking lot I slipped him the key to the room I'd rented earlier. I headed for the lounge, and they went upstairs. They both knew what they were there for.

Some of the girls had apartments that they rented for just that purpose. They always paid their own rent. I wanted them to feel that they were in business for themselves.

I encouraged them to work, but also to take care of themselves. I made sure that they were always clean and sanitary. I had a doctor on the South Side that I channeled them to if they needed an abortion. I kept them out of the gutter, made them feel that it was professionally good for them to work for me. I manipulated them to feel that they had potential, to raise the standard of their business dealings. I looked for their insecurities and used my personality to keep them emotionally attached to me with the promise of a good future for them. If they didn't want to stay with me, I let them go. There were always others I could find.

While they needed me for drugs and clientele, I didn't want to be their controller, their conqueror. I wanted to remain as out of sight as possible. So some of them had two apartments—one for hooking and another that they lived in. Many of them had children and a husband. Nobody was aware that the girls were working for me; people thought that I just knew them. And Connie didn't even know that much.

My marriage to Connie was in a separate compartment of my life. I don't think she ever knew about my girls—even toward the end. But she *did* know about my drugs. I wasn't even trying to hide them from her anymore. My growing need for heroin consumed my life.

At times the volcanic rage within me erupted. One day I sat at the kitchen table, preparing to shoot up. By now our second daughter, Elaine, had been born. Connie was in the bedroom taking care of her. Katie sat on the kitchen floor, watching what I was doing.

My veins had almost been destroyed. I jabbed the needle several times in an attempt to find an open one, but I couldn't get the blood up. And I knew that I couldn't push the plunger until I saw the blood.

Then the rage erupted. I yanked the needle out, ripping up my arm as I did so. I threw the needle across the room and headed for the bathroom.

When I came back out, Connie stood there crying.

She rarely cried in front of me, because she knew how violently upset I got at seeing tears.

"What's wrong with you?" I shouted at her.

"*This* is wrong!" she shouted back, waving the needle—still full of drugs—in my face.

"Give me that. How'd you get it?" I asked, grabbing for the needle.

"I'll tell you how I got it," she said. "Katie brought it to me! Asked me why her Daddy threw it!"

I looked at her, standing there holding the baby, Katie clinging to her legs. My rage gave way to guilt—crippling guilt greater than I'd ever felt before. It taunted me, consumed me, as it had the first few months after Mom died. Suddenly I saw Mom's face again, heard her saying, "Someday, Jimmy, you'll be sorry!"

I felt the dam about to break within me. I pushed Connie aside and fled out in the night.

My life went steadily downhill from then on. The guilt drove me to the drugs, even though the drugs increased the guilt. I couldn't push their faces out of my mind: Mom and Dad. My cousin, Dan, who had died of an overdose two years after I turned him on to drugs. My son, Scott, back down in Tennessee. My other son whose face I'd never seen. Connie, Katie, and Elaine. It seemed as though they all were pointing at me, chanting in unison, "Someday, Jimmy, you'll be sorry . . . sorry . . . sorry . . . s-o-r-r-y!"

I lost control more and more. I spent weeks at a time in hospital psych wards, in detox units, in drug rehabilitation centers. When I wasn't in the hospital, I was sitting in a jail cell, kicking my habit cold turkey with nothing to numb the guilt. For a time I could conceal my absences from work with false reports; but then, through insurance reports, they found out. They gave me a few chances to change at first.

I spent less and less time at home. I couldn't stand the pain of what I was doing to my family. It was tough on Connie. For the first time since early childhood, I became dependent on another person. I became weak, a different Jim than the one she'd married. She lost respect for me, and she lost affection. She said, "You've driven the love out of me!"

Sometime in 1968 or 1969 I met Joy. Her boyfriend was the millionaire owner of a variety-store chain. She was heavily into drugs and moved in a circle of affluent people. We developed a mutually dependent relationship that helped me through this time in my life.

We did drugs together. I supplied hers when she needed them, and she supplied mine. We were good business friends, but it went deeper than that. She became a good friend, a good lover, a good companion. She was always there when I needed her. She was like an island of safety in my disintegrating life.

In the fall of 1969 I lost my job with the consumer products company. My drug needs had become apparent to everyone. I couldn't control my dependence any longer.

Connie went back to work to bring some money in for food. She deeply resented me for what I had become. She tried as long as she could to help me, but she didn't know what to do. And I resented her! I hated being dependent on her. I resented the fact that she seemed to have her life so in control when my whole world had begun to collapse. I wouldn't *let* her help; I resented everything she tried to do for me.

I think I resented her most because I had so much guilt accumulating for the way I was hurting her and the girls. And every time she tried to help, it only caused more guilt.

Just before Christmas she confronted me with something new. "Who is Joy, Jim?" she asked one day.

"What do you mean, 'Who is Joy?'" I asked, trying to avoid the inevitable.

"She's the one who's always calling here, isn't she? She's your lover, isn't she?"

I saw the hatred in her eyes. I'd never seen it before, and it hurt. I did the only thing I knew how to do; I struck back. "Yah, what of it? *You* sure aren't very loveable anymore!"

"I'm leaving, Jim. I can't take anymore," she calmly told me.

She took the kids and spent Christmas at her mother's house. I went over to Joy's house, spent the holidays bombed with her.

Shortly after Christmas Connie came back. She wanted to give it one more try. I was willing to go through the motions, but it didn't work. I'd closed the door; I felt too vulnerable to her. I was determined even now, when I was so much out of control, to make it on my own. I had to find a way to shake the guilt, get myself back in control before I hurt them even more. But I had to do it alone!

She was still working to support the family, while I sat home shooting drugs. She got a neighbor a few blocks away to babysit the girls. She'd walk over with the kids in the morning and then walk on to work. By then I'd lost my car too. The cops had impounded it on one of their successful drug busts.

At night I walked the few short blocks to pick up Katie and Elaine and bring them home. I could carry Elaine, but Katie had to walk. It was winter, and the streets were filled with slushy snow. We were so poor that we couldn't buy the girls boots. Katie had to wear worn-out tennis shoes.

One day as we walked home she began to cry. I stopped and looked down at her. She grabbed my hand and looked up at me with tear-filled eyes.

"Daddy, my feet are wet. I need boots, *I need boots!*" she pleaded with me.

Her innocent, pleading eyes burned my soul. She penetrated through my self-protective walls to where I still could feel. And like a knife plunged deep into my flesh, then twisting in an ever-widening circle of pain, her look cut me in a new and deeper way than any other pain ever had. I'd hurt others before, but most of them were able to take care of themselves. Katie was my little daughter, dependent on me, her father, to protect her from danger. And I was her biggest enemy; *I was hurting her the most!* From that moment on, I never spent a moment without agonizing guilt and pain. Not even booze or drugs could mask the agony any longer!

Sometime in the middle of January Connie moved back in with her folks. I was alone, all alone. Even though a part of me wanted and needed that isolation—I felt that I could stay in better control alone—I wanted her to stay with me forever. But she left; she rejected me! I got her on her feet and then when I was down, she left me!

The dam broke within me again. The rage erupted, focusing on Connie. I took all my anger out on her. If I could have gotten my hands on her right then, I would have killed her. Instead, I harassed her constantly until finally she had to get a restraining order on me to protect her and the girls.

She was terrified of me, and with good reason. I was totally unpredictable. The monkey on my back had destroyed me, and in the wake of the self-destruction, I now tried to destroy Connie!

11. On the Skids

After Connie left, I stayed in the apartment on Waveland where we'd lived for several years. Within a couple of weeks, I'd turned it into a dope fiend's pad. Addicts on the street were always looking for a place to shoot up, and I figured it might as well be with me—at least we'd all have drugs. More dopies went in and out of my apartment than out of Grand Central Station.

Late one afternoon I ran into a couple of my dopie friends downtown.

"Hey, come on up to my place later," I suggested. "I just scored a big hit of smack."

One of them was a new friend by the name of Nick. He and I had struck up a useful friendship. He had a lot of good connections with crooked doctors who could get us drugs when we wanted them. He took me to their offices, introduced me to them. This greater access to pharmaceutical drugs such as Dilantin, morphine, and some of the heavy barbiturates just contributed to a faster decline in my ability to control my bondage.

I was quickly losing control again.

Early that evening Nick and a couple more dopies I knew came over. Together we shot most of the drugs I had on the coffee table.

Half-obliterated, I sat there looking around the room.

"Man, whatever have I come to?" I thought. I looked at the two dopies sitting across from me on the couch that Connie and I had bought together.

"If I weren't going down the drain, I'd never associate with guys like these," I thought. They were slime. They had dirty, long hair, bad breath, and broken teeth. They wore dirty, ragged clothes over their dirty, smelly bodies. They were there only to get their free fix at my expense. But how could I consider myself better?

Nick certainly wasn't any better. "At least he's my friend," I thought, staring at him as he nodded out across the room. But I wasn't even sure he was that! I had no reason to really trust him, and I sure would never let him in on any of my weaknesses. He was simply convenient to me, as I was to him.

Just then the phone rang. I stumbled for it, knocking it to the floor and almost falling myself as I reached down for it. At last I got it to my ear.

"Yah," I muttered into the receiver.

"Jimmy, is that you?"

I recognized my sister's voice. I hadn't heard from Fran for months, so I knew she wasn't making just a social call. I felt the panic begin to push its way to the surface from deep within.

"What's wrong?" I asked.

"Jimmy, it's Dad," she said. I caught the sound her voice had tried to hide.

"What's he done now?" I asked. I hadn't seen Dad in almost ten years. I hadn't written or phoned since returning to Chicago; I simply couldn't deal with the guilt I felt at having driven him crazy. But I knew that he still lived in his own little world down in Boliver, Tennessee, in the hospital.

Fran's voice brought me back to the present. "He's dead, Jimmy. He had a stroke and died early this morning."

Her words cut through my drug-induced stupor right into the very core of my being.

"Dead?" I dropped the phone. "Dead!"

"Hey, Jim, what's wrong?" Nick asked.

I walked into the bedroom, shut the door.

"Dead—he *can't* be dead!" I said out loud. My mind overflowed with mental images of my dad.

"Throw it harder, Jimmy, throw it harder," I heard him urge me. I saw the delight on his face the night he brought those new spike shoes to me. I remembered the Christmas he tried to show me how to use the bench press machine he had given me, and I laughed out loud at the memory.

Then my mind raced on to later times. "Why do you treat me that way, Jimmy?" I heard him asking. I saw his face the morning I walked in after having stolen his last five dollars. I remembered the times he told me about the "eye in the sky." I saw him on the day of Mom's funeral, with his blank, emotionless expression.

"Dead?" I thought. "I killed him years ago. It just took him this long to stop breathing."

Because I couldn't stand the silence of the room another minute, I went back to the living room. Nick had left, but the other two dopies were still on my couch.

I sat down in a chair. Even though I was high on drugs, I couldn't get the memories of Dad out of my mind. I looked again at the two dopies on my couch, and suddenly it was Connie and Katie sitting there.

"Connie, is that you?" I almost asked. Then I heard the sound of children laughing. It was Katie and Elaine, happily at play out near the kitchen.

"Is that my girls?" I called. "Come on in here and see Daddy!" I looked out toward the kitchen and noticed, in the hallway, the little crayon marks that Katie and Elaine had made in playing. Had those marks always been there?

Then the silence of the house was all I heard. The used needles on the table in front of me brought me back to the reality of my life. The dopies were still nodding out from the drugs we'd shot earlier.

"Man, I've completely lost my mind!" I exclaimed.

The memories rushed over me in a flood that I couldn't stop. Dad and me playing ball; Mom cooking supper; Connie and the girls fixing Thanksgiving dinner. Then the pain began again—I felt trapped by pain, bound by guilt, held captive to a bondage greater than even my need for drugs.

"It's no use—there's no hope!" I cried. I dissolved some pills, picked up a needle, and hit it.

When I woke up the next day no one else was there, and all my drugs were gone with my friends. All they had left me was the agony of my silent memories.

I knew that I had to get some drugs. The agony was just too great. But I was broke, completely without any money. When my mind couldn't seem to function, and I couldn't come up with a quick scheme to get some cash, I started to panic.

The only person in the world that I thought I could get money from was Connie. Ordinarily I knew she would turn me down flat. But with Dad's death I thought I could con her out of some.

I walked the few blocks to where she worked and asked her for twenty dollars. "Connie, I gotta go to Dad's funeral. Please let me borrow twenty to get a bus ticket," I begged.

"You just want it to get high," she accused me. I'd burned her so many times before.

"Please, Connie, Dad's dead. *Please* help me get to the funeral!" I pleaded with her several times. Finally, just to get rid of me, she handed me the twenty.

"At least he won't be able to see the creep that you've become!" she shouted at me, turning away repulsed.

I stuffed the money in my pocket. I felt like dirt for conning her out of her money. I had no intention of going to Tennessee to the funeral. I needed a fix, and I needed it fast.

I went to see a crooked doctor I knew, who gave me a prescription for Dilantin. After I got my drugs from a druggist, I went over to Joy's house. I needed to forget that phone call the night before. I needed to forget going to Tennessee for the funeral, because I couldn't leave my drug sources. I couldn't risk being caught without the fix I needed—especially in Tennessee!

I sat with Joy for many hours, drinking booze and listening to her Diana Washington records. When she finally passed out from all the booze, I went through her purse and took all the drugs and money I could find. I found her car keys too and took off in her car. I could now afford to make a *real* drug buy.

I didn't get far. Either I passed out or blanked out, but I ran smack dab into the back of a truck and totaled the car.

Joy couldn't believe that I had stolen her car and wrecked it. "That's it, Jim," she told me. "I've had it up to here with your sick tricks. Don't expect me to put up with you any longer."

I'd burned her so often and so deeply that she would rather I stayed away from her. Once she had needed me, been dependent on me—and now, when I needed her the most, she turned her back just as Connie had! Just as everyone had!

I remembered how Dad had done the same thing to me.

I don't need *any* of you, I thought. I don't need anybody or anything. But I did. Deep within, in the center of my pain-filled soul, I was crying out for help. But the only help I could find was at the end of a needle. I was going down the tubes, had turned into a cold-blooded snake. And I didn't know how to stop the fall.

In the early part of 1970 I could still supply my own drugs with crooked scams. I had met a fellow by the name of Jack who was up on all the drugs. He introduced me to a book called the PDR (Physician's Desk Reference)—showed me how to read it and taught me the benefits of using it.

With the help of the PDR I learned how to convince a doctor to write me a prescription for Class A narcotics. I now knew the right things to say, the symptoms to describe, and the illnesses to claim I'd been diagnosed with. I even knew what side effects to fake in order to get the doctor to prescribe harder drugs.

In addition to the edge it gave me with a doctor, the PDR also helped me with my own prescription-writing. It kept me from an overdose and taught me which drugs I could mix and which combinations to avoid. To me it was a matter of survival. I knew I'd never escape my drug bondage. But I still hoped that I could manage the addiction.

Yet I *couldn't* manage. My life was on the skids, driven there by the guilt of my silent memories.

I had a big box of pictures that I often sat and looked at for hours. Pictures of times with Mom and Dad in Tennessee. Pictures of me with Connie and the girls. Me, dressed up in a suit getting into my company car. Me, accepting golf trophies. The pictures drove me nuts.

On Christmas Eve of 1970 I sat looking through the pictures once again, all alone in my lonely apartment. "Man, I've blown it all—I've blown it all!" I said aloud. I walked over to a mirror and looked at the image staring back at me. I couldn't believe the animal I'd become. The eyes that stared back at me were lifeless, completely without feeling or life.

I sat back down beside the pictures. I picked up one of Connie and me, arms around each other, with Katie and Elaine sitting on the floor in front of us, and the agony of how I'd hurt them settled in once more.

"I'm so sorry. God, I'm so sorry!" I cursed out loud. Maybe it wasn't a curse—but a cry for help. But no one heard. I grabbed a pair of scissors and cut myself out of the picture.

From that day on I started slowly cutting up the pictures. First the ones of me. Then those of people I'd hurt. Soon that box of pictures was nothing but the shreds of my broken life.

It seemed to me that 1970 was the worst year of my life. I had lost control. In fact, I'd lost everything that had ever meant anything to me. Everybody I cared about was gone. I couldn't make things happen anymore. I couldn't blank out the pain anymore. I was totally alone—haunted by painful guilt on my way down to the pit of hell. Trapped! Unable to do a thing to stop my fall!

12. Call the Wagon on This Scum!

King Heroin is my shepherd, I shall always want. He maketh me to lie down in the gutters. He leadeth me beside the troubled waters. He destroyeth my soul. He leadeth me in the paths of wickedness. Yea, I shall walk through the valley of poverty and will fear no evil, for thou, Heroin, art with me. Thy needle and capsule comfort me. Thou strippest the table of groceries in the presence of my family. Thou robbest my head of reason. My cup of sorrow runneth over. Surely heroin addiction shall stalk me all the days of my life, and I will dwell in the house of the damned forever.

Found in a car beside a dead heroin addict
near Reedsville, North Carolina.

Something woke me, and I sat up straight in the bed. The clothes I still wore from the night before were wet with sweat. My pillow was also soaked—with sweat, or tears, I wasn't sure which.

I swung my legs over the side of the bed, sat up, and put my head in my hands. "God, it hurts so bad!" I said to no one. My head throbbed with pain; my stomach rolled with nausea and the heaves. I headed for the bathroom.

Later I fell back into bed. But sleep wouldn't come and rescue me from the wretched realization of the man I had become. I lay there motionless, yet torn apart by the torrent of emotions ripping me apart inside. I was coming unglued—totally and hopelessly out of control! I didn't know how to get out of the situation I was in. There wasn't hope for me—anywhere!

I sat up again, walked over to the window, and stared out into the blackness of the night.

"It's no use. There's no hope!" Silently my mouth formed the words. I turned back to the bed and reached under the pillow for my outfit. But the drugs were gone—I'd shot them all.

I stumbled out of the bedroom to the living room, knowing that there was a bottle of whiskey out there. I saw it on the floor and grabbed it desperately, but it was empty.

"Damn!" I shouted, throwing the bottle across the room. It shattered into a million pieces, just like my life! I searched all over the apartment, but there was nothing. Nothing to stop the replaying of my memories and the pain I felt. Nothing to deaden the pain of withdrawal.

I headed back to the bedroom. I'd just come off a six-week stay at Bridwell Jail for possession of narcotics. When I was released, they had handed me a little shaving kit. It was still in the bag I had carried home with me. I had already used the thirty dollars they gave me, to cop a fix on the way home. But the shaving kit was there.

I tore it open, looked inside at a razor, some shaving cream, a bar of soap, a comb, and a little bottle of rubbing alcohol. That was all I had.

"Gotta get rid of the shakes," I said, unscrewing the cap on the rubbing alcohol. I turned the bottle up, guzzling the whole thing before I could get a taste.

I fell back on the bed. It was useless; it didn't stop the pain.

"No use — no hope for me!" I mumbled to myself, over and over, as I lay there rocking on my side, trying to evade the silence of my memories.

It was this way night after agonizing night. My habit had destroyed the exterior of my life, and now it was turning inward, to wage its last stand on my soul, my very life!

About the only things I had left of what used to be were the box of cut-up photographs and several golf trophies I had kept. I couldn't bear to part with them. But I couldn't bear to see their constant reminder of what I'd lost, either, so they lay in a pile on a closet floor.

I rummaged through them now. Maybe there was a bag of smack still hidden with them. I pulled a trophy out and sat on the floor looking at it. "Presented to Jim Dycus, 1967 Low Net Player."

I thought back to the day I'd won that trophy. Man, I played my best round ever that day! I remembered. I also remembered the new golf outfit I'd worn, the fifty-dollar Etonic golf shoes I'd bought for the occasion, and the golf clubs that were my prized possession. I'd hocked them long ago to put a needle in my arm.

I stumbled over to the mirror and stared at myself. "I'm not even the same man anymore!" I said aloud. I was down to less than 130 pounds — just skin and bones. My looks were gone. My checks sank in, and my hard, unfeeling eyes seemed to haunt the image in the mirror. I was dirty and smelly, my long beard and hair greasy and stringy.

The trip down memory lane ended as I faced the reality staring out

At only three years of age, I already looked through skeptical eyes—determined to challenge anything or anyone who kept me from having my own way. Chicago, 1942.

Mom, Dad, and me on the front steps of our northside Chicago "walkup" apartment in 1945. This was taken when Dad was still a successful middle-class businessman.

Mom and Dad always dressed me in suits and nice clothes. Dad would tell me, "Jimmy, keep your hair, teeth, fingernails, and shoes clean and shiny all the time." Chicago, 1947.

Dad and I shared a special closeness in my early childhood years. This picture was taken during one of our Tennessee summer vacations—days that even now bring happy memories. Tennessee, 1948.

I was ten or eleven here, busy with baseball and boy scouts and childhood friends, before drugs caused a corrupt change in my personality. Chicago, 1950.

Dad had stopped drinking and had gone back to church when this picture was taken in Chicago, 1953. I remember seeing him read his Bible and pray. But not long after this, he began hearing voices and seeing his "eye in the sky."

At sixteen, already sporting tattoos and experimenting with drugs, I thought my life was "cool" and that everything was under control. Little did I realize the bondage I was headed for. Chicago, 1955.

Always the ham, I didn't realize how soon drugs would take the fun out of my life. Dad sits in the background— the wall of bitter emotions already separating us. Chicago, 1956.

By the time this picture was taken, I was twenty, completely bound to heroin, and living the blackest years of my life. Dad and I lived in two different worlds. Tennessee, 1959.

After Dad was admitted to the state hospital, Mom's father (on her right) and her brother Claude helped her through the difficult months before her death. Tennessee, 1959.

Chicago Teen Challenge. This forbidding exterior greeted me on 20 January 1972. But on the following day, inside where warmth and love reached me, I gave my life to God. Immediately, he proclaimed me "Not Guilty!"

Ken Schmidgall, the director of Chicago Teen Challenge, acted as my spiritual father. His aggressive kindness gave me hope for the first time in fifteen lonely years. Chicago, 1972.

On 2 June 1973 in Chicago, Barb and I began our life together. That day I determined to be the man God knew I could be.

My son two week old Jimmy held by me. It seemed as though I'd waited forever for an answer to my prayer for a son. At last God knew I could be the father Jimmy would need. Chicago, 1978.

Paster George Cope became my first Senior Pastor as I entered the ministry early in 1979. He also became my friend. We spent six years in full-time ministry together at Belmont Assembly of God. Chicago, 1979.

Here, I am ministering to single adults in 1987. Every time I stand before a congregation to preach or teach, I am filled with joy at God's transforming grace and power.

Jimmy and Jackie posing with Daddy in Chicago, 1981. What a privilege to be a father and share childhood with my children!

My son Scott and I had this picture taken during his first visit with us in Chicago, 1983. God gave both of us the miracle gift of restoration and love between father and son.

Dinah, Jackie, and Jimmy—these, my three youngest children, are a special joy, and have willingly accepted Daddy, past and all. Casselberry, Florida, 1987.

Barb and me with our son, Jimmy, and our daughters Dinah (left) and Jackie in Casselberry, Florida, 1988. The bondage of my guilt has been transformed by grace into new life. God has set the captive free.

at me from that mirror. By this time every fiber of my being was crying out for a fix.

"Gotta make a score," I mumbled. "Gotta get a fix!"

I looked around the room. All I had left worth pawning was a color television set. I knew that I couldn't get it down the steps alone, so I stumbled down the steps and across the alley to the apartment Nick had rented. "Hey, Nick, help me get my TV down the steps. I gotta take it down to Wilson Avenue and hock it for a fix," I told him.

I had the keys to a car that belonged to a waitress I'd shacked up with the night before. I'd driven her to work and said I'd pick her up.

We went back up the steps to my place. Mike, another kid that Nick knew from his building, came along. They helped me get the TV down and loaded in the trunk of the car.

We headed south on Western Avenue, the tied-down trunk lid bouncing against the TV. Wilson was just a few blocks away, and it had rows of pawn shops where I knew I could pawn the TV for a hundred bucks. We turned west on Wilson.

"Damn, there's O'Leary!" Nick exclaimed from the driver's seat. He was in better shape than me so he was driving. O'Leary was a narcotics cop who had busted us many times. He saw us now, in a car he didn't know, with a television hanging out the trunk. He passed us going east, and as we watched, he made a U-turn and headed in our direction. He turned on his flashing lights.

We had a vial of pills in the car with us. "Quick, swallow these!" I cried, giving Mike and Nick each a handful. I swallowed the rest of them and threw the empty vial under the seat. I knew the cops would find it, but they couldn't bust us for an empty vial.

"Pull over!"

O'Leary and his partner got out with their guns drawn. They called us out and frisked us. Then O'Leary shook down the car for drugs while his partner kept us spread against the car.

O'Leary was furious when he found that the car was clean. "What'd you do, scarf them?" he yelled, shaking the empty vial in my face.

He called the car in and seemed disappointed to find that it wasn't reported stolen.

"Where'd you steal the TV?" he asked next.

"Man, it's mine!" I told him.

"Can't be yours," he said. "You ain't got nothin' but the tracks all over your arms and legs!"

I felt like screaming back, "Yah, and these tracks lead to the tracks where Mom died!" but I didn't. He wouldn't care. *Nobody* did.

O'Leary motioned to our car. "Get in," he told Nick and me. "My partner's driving you in."

Mike started to climb in too. "Nah, not you. You're coming with me," O'Leary told him, motioning with his hand back to the squad car. He pulled his handcuffs out and cuffed Mike's arms behind him.

O'Leary and Mike got to the station before us. When we walked in, Mike was sprawled on the floor, groaning, blood pouring from his nose.

"He slipped and fell," O'Leary explained with a shrug.

We knew that was a joke! O'Leary had busted him one right in the nose.

"Shake the car down again," O'Leary told the cops standing there with him.

They went out to search the car. When they came back, they had about an ounce of heroin, needles and all!

"Hey, O'Leary, look what we found in the car!" one of the cops said, smiling. Nick and I knew that the car had been clean. They'd put the drugs there themselves.

We protested, of course, but they arrested us on drug possession charges. We sat in the county jail a couple of weeks waiting for the court date. I knew that I had a loophole this time—the drugs had been a plant—but I didn't know if it would be enough.

Our day in court finally arrived. When I went before the judge, I didn't wait for the public defender to speak for me. "Judge, they didn't find any drugs the first time they they shook us down," I told him. "But when they got us to the station they decided to do a second search. *Then* they said they found some heroin. Besides that, the kid with us rode to the station with O'Leary in the squad car. Somehow he had an 'accident' and broke his nose. How'd *that* happen?"

The judge didn't want any trouble with my case. All he wanted to do was expedite it and get on with the next one. "Discharged," he said, and I was free to walk out.

I headed back home to my apartment. When I got there, I discovered that O'Leary had conducted a search of that too. My golf trophies lay kicked and broken all over the place. My box of cut-up pictures had been turned upside down and dumped in a scattered heap in the middle of the floor.

As I stooped to pick them up, the top picture—a shred with Katie's face smiling up at me—caught my eye. Her happy four-year-old smile seemed so out of place in my world now. I threw the pictures down, kicked the pile of shreds.

"It's gone!" I thought, "it's gone. My life is gone! Man, I'm not living—I'm dying in the pit of hell!"

I headed out to cop a fix.

I didn't have any decent friends left. I looked like a bum on the street, and that's who I associated with. No one else would have anything to do with me. When I walked through town, women took their children across the street to avoid walking past me. Well-dressed men put their hands in their pockets and gripped their wallets tightly as they hurried by. And with good cause. My bondage to drugs guaranteed one thing: every day, every couple of hours, I needed to jab another needle in my overused veins. Whatever I had to do to fill that vial with dope, that's what I did!

Many of my drug sources were on the South Side of Chicago. Most people—even dopies—wouldn't go down to that black area to cop a fix. But I often did. Other times I got my drugs from dopies in the uptown area of Chicago. One of the uptown dopies that I met up with was Lenny Slade, a notorious dealer in the Irving Park–Broadway area. Lenny made me look like an amateur. He was superaggressive, and no one crossed him twice. He took double-crossers out first.

Years ago Lenny had had a wife and kid and a nice apartment, but he had blown it all! Maybe that's why we hit it off in the beginning. I started running around with him. Nick didn't like Lenny, so I left Nick behind. Lenny was a good source of drugs for me, and because he was so notoriously bad, he offered protection in a way, a covering.

But dopies don't really become friends. They just use each other to serve their own purposes. That's the kind of relationship we had.

Soon I got tired of his using me, using my drugs. Although I still shared his when they were offered, I quit giving him any. Lenny knew a Chevrolet dealer who let us use his rental cars. Since Lenny had no license, I used my phony driver's license to get the car. Lenny often took the car to make his drug buys. I stopped him from doing that now too. That meant the end of his free ride to deliver his drugs to his customers.

Lenny was furious that I'd crossed him. He called me on the phone: "Man, Dycus, you're gonna pay for this one!" he threatened me.

I was too sick of him to really care about his threats. I knew he meant business, but I did too. "I'm tired of your freeloading off my stuff, tired of your using my car," I told him. "You ain't gonna get any more from me!"

"Damn it, Dycus, I'm gonna take you out for that!" he yelled into the phone, then hung up.

When the threat sank in, his words made my blood run cold. I knew that if I was going to catch my lunch from anyone, he was the one capable of doing it.

Later that day I ran into another dopie I knew. "Hey, Dycus," he called. "Lenny's looking for you. He's got a gun and he's gonna kill you if he finds you!"

That I was concerned is an understatement. I lay low that night. But the next day I needed more drugs. I *had* to go cop some more, so I went over to a dealer's house.

"Hey, did you hear what happened to Lenny?" he asked.

I felt the sweat break out on my brow. I put my hand in my pocket to touch the cold steel of the revolver I carried with me. It gave me a sense of security as I asked, "What happened?"

"His exwife took him out last night," my connection told me.

I breathed a sign of relief. But as I thought about Lenny I wondered, "Will my life end like that?" Lenny and I were alike in so many ways, after all. He'd lost his wife and kid, just as I'd lost Connie and the girls. The monkey on his back had turned against him too. Even though he was notorious and feared, inside he was a lonely, bitter man who had no way to get rid of the pain his bondage gave him. Just like me!

By now I didn't even have a home anymore. I couldn't pay for anything but my drugs. I'd really hit the skids.

I went down to the Volunteers of America and got a bed in the dormitory there. They put me to work sweeping out the garage, loading trucks, helping pick up donations, doing whatever else they needed done. They paid only a dollar a day, but sometimes people gave me tips. Generally I'd have a couple of bucks at the end of the day — enough to buy a couple of pints of wine. I'd go sit on the railroad tracks behind the dorm and drink my wine.

Some nights I'd stare up and down those tracks, wondering where they came from, where they were going. In my drunkenness I'd try to focus on the tracks, way down as far as I could see. I wondered what I'd do if suddenly I saw Dad approaching. But I knew it'd never happen. He was gone—in the other direction.

"I wonder where the end is?" I'd ask myself. "Where will I wind up?"

Sometimes when I heard a train whistle, the horrors of those last few months I spent in Tennessee would swallow me up in grief. The sight of those tracks where Mom died, the sound of her bones being crushed by that engine, and the futility of that 100-step walk to her grave where I would beg for forgiveness taunted me.

Now, today, I wonder if I wasn't just testing fate by sitting on those tracks. I had nowhere else to go, no one else who wanted me. Maybe I could get rid of my guilt the same way that Mom had found an end to her pain. Only I didn't have enough guts to step in front the way she did. Maybe I thought I could drink enough to pass out on the tracks. I know that by that time, I didn't care how my life ended.

I did this every night for a couple of months, listening to a tiny transistor radio I had found and drinking until I felt like I had to go to sleep. Then I'd go back to the dorm and crawl in bed. If I was drunk enough, the bedbugs and cockroaches didn't bother me too much. And the wine stilled the silent memories that haunted my sleep each night.

One night, as I was walking to the store to get my wine, I saw Connie's car parked at a hot dog stand across the street. She was sitting in the passenger's seat—so who was she with? I looked toward the stand and saw some guy in a suit getting hot dogs. I felt the wrath boil up inside—how could she be with someone else?—but I knew I had to keep my control or I'd wind up back in jail. And I didn't want that.

I walked up to the car and, to my surprise, she rolled down her window. I saw the look of apathy turn to terror on her face as I stuck my head inside, close to her. She pulled back, fearful and repulsed.

"Better be careful, Connie," I said softly. "If I decide to, I'll kill him, and you too!" She knew I was capable of doing just that. She also knew that I rarely made a threat that I didn't carry out.

I pulled my head out and walked away. Somehow the terror on her face had relieved the pain I felt inside.

The day before Christmas all the work at the Volunteers of America was over. I stole a few bucks to rent a room in a hotel when I left the dorm. I also stole a bottle of Dolophine from one of the other men and shot it all in my rented room. The hotel kicked me out when I became disruptive. It was Christmas, and for me there was no room in the inn. No room anywhere.

It was twenty below zero, and the wind chill made it even colder. My left shoe had a hole in it, and my feet felt frozen. To make matters worse, I was coming down off the Dolophine.

I spotted a Salvation Army dropbox up ahead. I knew that if I could squeeze my way inside, I could cover up with the clothes it contained. I didn't even care about the rats that were probably in there. I opened the door and inched my way through the slot. Once inside, I got one of the biggest scares in my life.

"Yeow! Who are you?" I heard someone shout. Some half-bombed wino was already there! By morning we were both laughing about the scare we had given each other. But I wasn't laughing inside. As I lay there, I realized that I was as much a bum as that wino there with me.

Here I am, I thought. Just look at me now! I thought about the closets full of suits and ties I used to have. The tailor-made shirts, with hankies and cufflinks to match. The expensive shoes that lined the floor. All the things I used to have.

That's me, I thought as I looked at the sleeping wino. I'm a has-been just like him. Laying under layers of junk clothes in a Salvation Army dropbox to keep warm. I hadn't brushed my teeth in weeks, hadn't shaved in months, and my breath smelled foul from drugs and booze.

That night I did something I'd never done before. I turned my back to the bum beside me. I made it a practice never to turn my back on anyone, never to let my defenses down. But that night I didn't care. And silent tears flowed from my eyes for hours.

Although during my days with the Volunteers I had survived on booze alone, I was soon desperate for other drugs, and I got them any way I could. I started getting careless and taking chances. I even held up the same drugstore two times, just a couple weeks apart.

One day I was shacked up with a girl I had met in a bar. She offered me whiskey, but she didn't have any dope.

God, I gotta get some dope! I thought, pacing up and down in her shabby, run-down apartment. I looked at the mantel and my eyes fell on her cigarette lighter. It was one of those lighters that look like a gun.

"Come on," I told her, grabbing it off the mantel. "Let's take a ride."

I drove to a drugstore that I'd come to think of as my lucky charm. It was the same drugstore that I'd hit twice before in the past few weeks, and each time I'd walked out with a bag of narcotics.

"Stay here. I'll be right back," I said, walking in.

It was right before closing time, and no customers were inside. I walked back to the pharmacy counter where the clerk was working alone.

I opened my jacket so that he could see the "gun." "Give me all your Class A narcotics!" I told him.

He took a quick look at my face and then his eyes fell on the gun. He went to the refrigerator, filled a bag with vials of drugs, and handed it to me.

As I started to back my way up to the front, I heard a hard, cold voice that sent chills up my spine: "Halt or I'll shoot!"

In terror, I realized that the cops had staked the drugstore out!

For some reason I wheeled around instead of merely raising my arms. The cop fired, his bullet grazing my forehead and parting my hair. I fell to the floor on my knees, my head resting in my hands. As I opened my eyes, I felt the blood running through my fingers and down my arms. I looked at the floor and saw two pools of blood beneath my elbow.

This is it—this is the end! I thought.

I don't know how long I knelt there, but my life passed before my eyes. All the buried memories burst forth in a torrent of pain inside my head that was worse than the burning wound on my forehead. I saw Mom's finger pointing at me. I saw the tears flowing down Katie's little cheeks as she pleaded, "Please, Daddy, I need boots!" Face after face flashed in front of me. But I was too empty to even cry. Only the blood from my wound fell down my cheeks.

The cop's voice broke in on my silent pain.

"Call the wagon on this scum," he called.

The word penetrated through my pain. Suddenly I knew the cop was right. *Scum!* I thought. That's it! I've become scum! The scum of the earth. Look at me, world. Here's the scum of the earth. I'm as low as anyone can go.

13. Peanut Butter Therapy

It was February 22, 1971, when I was shot by that policeman's bullet. The paddy wagon picked me up and took me to Cook County Hospital to be stitched up, then deposited me in a holding cell at Cook County Jail. As I rode in that wagon I came face to face with the Jim Dycus I had become.

"Scum—that cop called me *scum!*" The word twisted round and round in my mind. It hurt worse than the physical pain I'd felt when I'd missed a vein and shot drugs into my muscles. It exploded, burned white hot; it seared me with its blazing truth.

I thought about Connie, recalled her repulsed, terror-filled eyes the night I'd stuck my face threateningly inside her car. I felt repulsed like that myself now.

"I really am a slimeball now," I thought. When I shut my eyes, my head throbbed with the pain. "Not even death wants me yet," I mumbled to myself.

The next day my case was continued until the 24th of March. On that day it was continued until the 30th, when I finally had my day in court.

The bailiff called my name and ushered me into the bullpen to await my turn to go before the judge.

"Listen, Dycus," he said to me, "you can get off with just a little bit of time if you want to plead guilty to theft instead of being tried or bound over to the grand jury for armed robbery."

I was cocky, sure of my ability to get out of this mess, and I laughed at his suggestion. "Man, they ain't got nothin' to keep me for!" I said. "They didn't find no gun on me. All I had was a cigarette lighter!"

I saw the look of disgust on the bailiff's face. He looked at me, then down at my record. "Hey man, this says you had a 45!" he shot back, shaking the papers in my face.

My cockiness vanished as the reality of my situation suddenly hit me. I'd been up on charges many times before, and my court savvy told me that one of two things had happened: either the bailiff was lying, or the narcs had planted a gun on me. I remembered drug plants in the past and knew that it wasn't uncommon for a plant to take place. Then I remembered the cops' words as I lay on the ground after my bust: "Call the wagon on this scum!" I knew where they thought scum belonged, and every instinct in me told me that my time was up—I was headed for a jail sentence.

I pleaded guilty to the lesser charge of theft. "Nine months in County Jail," the judge called out, pounding with his gavel on the desk.

The cell door locking behind me echoed the sound his gavel had made. I'd done time before, but somehow this time seemed different. I was one of the hardened, experienced addicts this time. And yet within me my defensive walls seemed to be crumbling into dust.

At times I kept the crumbling defenses from showing. I laughed along with all the others at the Salvation Army workers who came to talk with us. I scorned their message and walked away from their offer of a friendly conversation.

I even held my own among the other inmates. Homosexual activity was a big problem in the jail, as I learned one day when a big black dude hit on me for sex.

I was supposed to be working in the laundry (that's where they put all the addicts) on a Monday morning. I'd managed to buy some pills from one of the other inmates and had taken them over the weekend. Now I was crashing, and I was too sick to work. Instead, I lay on my cot. No one else was on the tier except Ray.

Ray was the "barn boss" on our tier—that is, his job was to sweep the tier—so he had access to all the cells at certain times. He was the meanest dude in the jail, noted for hitting on the young boys and forcing them to give him sex.

Ray walked into my cell that morning and sat down on my cot, closer than I wanted him to be. "Hey, Dike, how about getting it on with me?" he asked with a leer.

As he spoke those words, fear gripped me. I knew that the next two minutes in that cell with Ray would demand all the strength and courage I could muster.

Even though I was shaking in my boots, I looked him straight in the eyes. Without moving a muscle I said in a low, even voice, "No, you're not going to do anything to me. You'll have to kill me first!"

I remember the silence after I spoke. I had resolved that I was going to let him beat me—until I couldn't walk, if that's what it took. A guard would eventually come to help, I hoped. Now I waited.

But Ray just sat there looking at me for what seemed to be an eternity. Then without a word he slowly stood up, turned his back to me, and walked out. He backed off and never bothered me again. My stand was accepted and respected by the other inmates.

But then late at night, alone in my cell, I'd face the memories and guilt that had put me there. They were a far stronger adversary than Ray; they refused to leave me alone.

If only somehow I could avoid the pain my life has brought, I thought, wishing I could turn the clock back to a happier time. But I couldn't. I'd become the scum that no one wanted.

"Someday you'll be sorry, Jimmy—someday!" I heard my mother's voice. Without the drugs to stop the pain and cover up the guilt, my life became a nightmare. Those nine short months became an eternal bondage to my pain.

I was utterly alone. No one visited; no one called. And inmates don't make friendships. Each one spends his time walled up within his own silent hurt.

I couldn't stop the memories from taunting me, but the pressure of my life in jail caused almost as much terror. I went to sleep every night wondering if I'd wake up in the morning or be stabbed during the night. I shut my ears to the sounds around me. I kept my grip on sanity by playing the mind games I'd learned to play so well. And I counted the days to my release.

When I was released I had nowhere to go. I headed for the Salvation Army Men's Social Service Center, where I knew I could at least get three hots and a cot. They put me to work sweeping out the furniture warehouse. Because of my physical deterioration, however, I couldn't even do that!

My pain and guilt had bound me to an emotional addiction far greater than any physical dependence I had on drugs. Jail and my enforced withdrawal had wiped out any *physical* need for drugs. But I craved them so that I could smother the guilt. Yet I couldn't get rid of the guilt, couldn't suppress it any longer even *with* drugs. But because drugs were the only comfort I'd known in years, they were the comfort—cold comfort—I now sought.

I still knew a handful of doctors who would give me a prescription for drugs. I still had a few scams for getting enough money to buy them. So I began another vicious cycle of doing drugs, getting busted, drying out in a hospital or at the Salvation Army, then going out for more drugs. I couldn't control my life; I couldn't manage it without drugs, and I surely couldn't manage it with them.

The Salvation Army helped me join a government-sponsored methadone program, a maintenance program that was supposed to give me the chance to lead a normal life. All I had to do was check in two or three times a week and pick up my tablets of methadone, the "miracle drug" for heroin addicts.

But the program failed utterly. I was the same man I'd always been, wracked with the same painful memories and guilt. When I looked in the mirror, cold, lifeless eyes stared back at me. I still had flashbacks, still heard my mother's voice, still lay helpless night after night while all the faces of the people I had hurt paraded through my mind.

I broke the program, left the Army, and went back out on the streets. But it was the middle of winter, and I had nowhere to go. I remember the day I left. I pulled my shabby, oversized coat around me to try to get some relief from the twenty-below-zero wind blowing across the icy Chicago streets. I reached up to yank the ragged ski cap down over my dirty long hair. My greasy beard had icicles forming on it from the drips falling from my nose. Jamming my hands through the holes in my pockets and wadding up the lining in my clenched fists, I turned my back to the wind.

Soon one shoe fell off and I fell to the ground. The shoes were several sizes too big for me, but I had wadded newspapers around my feet. I jammed my foot back in the shoe, struggled to my feet, and stumbled on down the street.

As I turned the corner, I saw a sign that read, "Salvation Army Men's Social Service Center." I had managed only to go around the block! I stumbled through the door and felt the warmth of the lobby.

"I gotta get out of the cold!" I said to the man sitting at the desk.

"Sorry, we're filled up tonight," he replied, without lifting his head to look at me.

Panic hit me. I knew I'd reached the end of my rope. "I *can't* go back out there!" I told him.

"Sorry, fella," was his answer to me.

I stood looking at him for what seemed like hours. Still he never once even glanced my way.

I turned to look out at the cold winter street. What'll I do now? I wondered.

Just then another man walked up to the desk. I recognized Pete, the night manager. "What's happening?" he asked the desk clerk.

"No more room!"

Pete glanced at me—then out at the night—and touched my arm.

"Come on, buddy," he said to me. "We'll stick a cot up in the dorm for you." His kindness penetrated to my heart.

I fell down two more times as I shuffled to that cot. Pete half-carried me the last stretch. As I finally collapsed onto the cot, I was utterly helpless for the first time in my life.

I was withdrawing from methadone, the worst addiction in my thirteen years as a heroin addict. I was so weak I couldn't stand. My body was racked with chills and the shakes. My veins felt as if someone were using pliers to rip them out of my flesh. They had all been overused to the point of destruction from shooting anything and everything into them. And I was completely disoriented. I couldn't even follow a simple TV show or add ten plus ten.

The worst part of that night was the memories. My mind couldn't focus on any one thing. It was splintered by thousands of piercing memories. Each time I closed my eyes, another face that I had hurt would appear within my mind. I knew that I was in the pit of hell, and I didn't know how I would ever be able to get out.

I had thought that methadone, the drug cure of the seventies, was the thing that was going to get me through. It was supposed to free me forever. But I wasn't free! I didn't have to use heroin, but I wasn't free from the memories of the past, from the guilt I carried, or from the person I had become.

A cockroach ran up my arm as I lay on the cot. As I watched him crawling I thought, I ought to swat him off me, but he and I are brothers—we're just alike. I'm a human cockroach!

I saw myself like that, and I hated what I saw. Lying on that cot, I felt utterly hopeless. My strength and my motivation were gone. My body was riddled with pain; my mind was burned out. The sins of the past were upon me. That familiar feeling of bondage gripped me tighter than the bonds of the strait jackets I had felt in the past.

I didn't know what I was going to do, but I did know one thing:

I didn't want any more drugs! I reached up and grabbed the medal I wore around my neck. It didn't really mean anything to me, but it as a religious symbol of some kind. I hadn't cried out to anyone for help since childhood, but I had reached the place during that night where I realized I needed help. From the depths of my anguish I cried, "God help me, *God help me!*" I didn't know what kind of help I wanted. I didn't even know if there was really a God who *could* help me. Or who *would*! But I wanted desperately for my captivity to end. I tossed and turned all night, aching for an end to all my anguish.

In the morning I decided to go talk to the Center's director. I struggled up off that cot and shuffled to the bathroom. I was dirty and unshaven, and I felt the need to clean myself up.

I picked the razor up and stood looking in the mirror. I saw my dirty, greasy, long beard and knew that it had to go. When I glanced up at my eyes, I drew back in horror at what I saw. I saw the black rings first, then the bloodshot white inside the sunken holes. Man, I look terrible, I thought.

But then I looked inside the eyes. It was as though I saw into my very soul! I'd never seen anything so cold, so hard, so lifeless.

I threw the razor away, having never touched my face with it, and wrapped my head in a towel. When I yanked the towel away minutes later, I saw my face again in the mirror, and was again horrified by what I saw. I turned my back to that image in the mirror.

"It's a bummer!" I screamed. "Life's not even real—it's just a bummer!" At that moment I knew that I never wanted another needle in my arms, another pill to swallow, or another drug to ease my pain. *I wanted out!*

I walked into the office. "I need help," I pleaded with the director. "I don't know what, but I do know that I don't ever want any more drugs. Please, can you send me somewhere where someone can help me?"

He wrote a letter to send with me to the emergency room of Cook County Hospital. The letter said simply, "This is Jim Dycus. We've tried everything we know to do, and we can't reach him. He doesn't respond to anything. Can you help him?"

They didn't help. They gave me a shot of Valium to calm me down, but I knew it wasn't what I needed.

God, there's *no* one who can help! I thought.

"There's nothing we can do for you, buddy," the hospital attendant said. "You can stop on your way out and see a social worker if you want."

The social worker told me, "There's one program for drug addicts that you haven't tried. If you want to go, it's not very far from here."

I was desperate. "How can I get there? I'll try anything."

"Just give this to the cab driver," she told me, handing me a receipt.

Riding in that cab, I thought, *Another* program. Where's my life going? I can't live on drugs and I can't live without them. I can't face my memories, and I can't get rid of them.

The cab pulled up in front of an old mansion on Ashland Avenue. A big sign out in front read "Teen Challenge." Suddenly I felt like running, but I had no place to run. Besides, it was twenty below zero, and at least I'd be inside, out of the cold.

I walked up the steps, rang the doorbell. The door opened and a big, rough guy stuck out his hand. Instinctively I pulled back.

He laughed, grabbed my arm, and pulled me in. "Praise the Lord, brother!" he boomed.

Well I'd been in some weird situations before, but this took the cake. This guy was as rough as Lenny Slade. He had tattoos all over his body, and he was built like a fullback. As he held his arm out, I saw old tracks running up and down his arms. But he was smiling, and he said, "We're glad you're here."

I wondered why!

He took me into the office and began the initial interview with which I was so familiar. He introduced himself and started to tell me more about the place. As he talked, I heard the sound of a child playing out in the hall.

"Who's that?" I asked.

"Why, it's Mark, my son. He and my wife and other son are out in the living room."

I looked at him in surprise. "You're married?" I asked.

"Yes," he said. "I was a heroin addict for twelve years. But I've been clean for five years now." He smiled at me, leaned closer, and said, "Jim, Jesus could do the same thing for you!"

His words reached down inside my life of despair and found a little corner where a shred of hope still lived. That hope sprang up, burst forth, and brought with it a longing to believe what he was telling me—to believe what he *was*.

In all my years of drugs, I'd never met an addict who'd made it. One who'd found a way to break the bondage of addiction. Yet sitting here in front of me was one who claimed that he had. And he said that I could do the same.

Then I pulled myself back to reality. It's some kind of scam, I thought. There's no hope for me. He's trying to give me a snow job!

I remembered all the other hospitals, programs, and doctors who had tried to change my life before. I'd been through so many programs, talked to so many doctors, that I had them programmed. I knew just what to say, how to act, when to let them meddle.

But those doctors never got past my inner barricades to where the guilt was. They didn't even know it existed, so of course they never found a way to cure it. They couldn't offer anything that gave me hope of finding a way to deal with all the guilt I carried because of all the people I'd hurt. Or a way to end the nightly parade of pain that began with Mom's words: "Someday, Jimmy, you'll be sorry."

This exaddict named Stan sitting across from me now did. I felt those walls come tumbling down. Yet every bit of my street sense told me that the only way to survive was to tighten those walls back up—keep these people out.

Stan led me out to where several others were. As he introduced me, I began to retreat back inside. I didn't want to let these people in; I knew that I would feel too vulnerable if I did.

A little lady named Irene walked up to me. With her kind face beneath graying hair, she reminded me so much of Mom. She had one arm behind her back, and she smiled at me.

"Hi, Jim," she said, "I'm pleased to meet you. We're so glad you're here."

Man, I thought, I can't deal with all of this "nice guy" stuff. I turned away from her.

She walked around me so that I had to face her smile again.

"What do you want from me?" I snapped. "Just leave me alone!"

I watched her face as I spoke, expecting her to back off. That's what everyone else always did.

Instead, tears began to fall down her cheeks. She kept on smiling, though, and she stepped closer to me. She brought her tucked-back arm around in front and held out her hand to me.

I looked down to see what she had. There in her hand was a peanut butter sandwich.

"Take it," she said. "I thought you might be hungry." She thrust it in my hand and patted my arm maternally.

"I'm so glad you came," she repeated.

The rest of my walls came tumbling down!

I was still too ill from the methadone withdrawal to eat, but I clutched my sandwich as Stan took me upstairs and put me in a bed. I lay there shaking from the drugs all night, dozing off occasionally only to wake back up when the memory faces began to reappear.

Sometime later that evening I heard footsteps. Then men began to file into the room and surround my bed — six or eight of them. I didn't know what kind of trouble I was in for now. They grabbed each other's hands and began to pray: "God, we thank you for sending Jim Dycus to us. Please be with him, and let us help him find the hope he needs."

When I looked at their faces in the bright glow from the hall, I could tell that they were addicts, just like me. But they weren't on any high. Their steps were firm, their voices strong, and their eyes clear. To my surprise, I saw tears running down the faces of these great big guys — tears for *me!* They thanked God for me! They cried for me! I didn't know why they did that. Perhaps someone *did* care for me. I felt safe — and suddenly so very tired. I didn't want to run anymore. I fell asleep.

The next morning, as I lay in bed catnapping, I felt strangely peaceful. Even the shakes were gone. When I sensed that someone was looking at me, I slowly opened my eyes. Sitting on the foot of my bed was a great big smile! The man behind the smile had the kindest eyes I'd ever seen, and yet I felt as though he was looking right through me. I felt as though he could see my entire life with those eyes. I wanted to pull away, keep him out — and yet I felt drawn to him.

"Hi, Jim," he said. "I'm Ken Schmidgall."

He reached straight into my heart with his smile and friendly attitude as he sat there talking. He mentioned several different guys who'd been through this program. I even knew one of them from the streets! I'd never met a man like him before. He looked so naive and innocent. He had a bald head and a long nose. He was tall but slender — almost puny-looking! And he bubbled over with a joy and enthusiasm for life that I envied. I'd never met someone who was so aggressively kind to me before.

I heard a growing noise downstairs and looked at Ken inquiringly. He said, "The guys are having chapel. C'mon, let's go down."

I thought of how I looked. The night before Stan had suggested that I might like to take a shower. I knew that I probably smelled even worse than I looked. But I went down the steps with Ken.

As we walked into the chapel, I saw guys all over. A big black guy was lying flat on the floor. Others were standing, kneeling, lying all over—and all of them were praying out loud, all at the same time.

Man, what kind of place is this? I thought, sitting down in the chair closest to the door. A dark, foreign-looking guy—I later learned he was Spanish—was sitting next to me, his head in his hands.

All at once he stood up, raised his arms, and began to pray: "God," he cried, "I thank you for forgiving me for what I did to my mama!"

I sat up intently, and my spirit grabbed onto his words for all its worth. I felt tears well up inside. This Spanish guy had touched my heart with words that gave me hope—something I thought I'd lost forever.

For the first time in years I thought of Mom without seeing her finger pointing accusingly at me, without hearing her voice accuse me of my guilt. If God had forgiven that Spanish guy for what he did to his mom, whatever it was, maybe—just maybe—there was hope for me!

I felt a hand on my shoulder and looked up to see Ken standing there. "Jim," he asked, "do you want Jesus to forgive you for what you did to your mom?"

I leaped to my feet, grabbed his shirt, and doubled up my fist. "How did you know that?" I yelled.

He smiled at me and said, "Jim, if you want to start a new life, if you want to be forgiven, if you want to be healed of all the hurt and pain you're going through, *Jesus is the answer!*"

If I wanted! How I yearned to rid my life of all the guilt I had carried for so many years.

My tears fell freely for the first time in many years. I grabbed Ken's hand. "Yes, I want that!" I told him.

"All you have to do is tell him that you want him," Ken said. "Ask him to forgive you, and he'll do it."

I got down on my knees beside that folding chair. I didn't know how to pray or what to say. But I had to reach him, had to tell him that I wanted him to change my miserable life. "God, I don't know if you're real," I prayed. "I don't even know if you can do what these people say you can. But please, God, take away the pain! If you'll make me happy like these other guys, I'll do anything you want. I'll be anything you want me to be. I'll go anywhere you want me to go!"

I stayed there on my knees for a long time. Something was happening deep inside me, where I'd been dead for so many years. Feelings I hadn't felt since I was a little boy were rushing over me. Others that I had never felt and couldn't explain were bursting forth. I couldn't move, but I felt as if I was flying high, felt that nothing could pull me back down into my pain.

I got up feeling like Mr. Clean. The pain was gone! I felt free, light, released like a prisoner from bondage.

Ken laughed. I grabbed his collar. "Man, don't laugh at me!" I threatened.

He laughed again and hugged me. "I'm not laughing at you, Jim," he told me. "I'm happy for you. You're a new man! *You're free, Jim, free of pain!*"

14. Guilt to Grace

Even though the miracle of new life came to me instantly as I knelt there on that chapel floor, the transformation wouldn't be complete for several months.

Here I was, thirty-one years of age, and I had to abide by the rules for the first time in my life. I had followed few rules in my life as far back as I could remember. What rules I had obeyed were backed by the threat of force at the hands of uncaring or openly hostile jail guards, or came from unsympathetic hospital attendants or social workers.

Now I had people telling me what to do — and enforcing their rules with love! That was a combination I couldn't resist. The rules weren't too bad, although they made me feel like a kid again. No smoking, no drinking, no outside calls without permission. You couldn't leave the house without a staff member, and you couldn't even get a pass to leave attended until you'd been there for a month. You had to attend the classes, the prayer meetings, and the chapel services. You had to go to church when they said go.

It didn't sound too bad at first. But soon I realized the difference between just following the rules and living the life. The staff and some of the guys who'd been there awhile were having a great time with all this church stuff. But the rest of us were just trying to play the game, just going through the motions. That wasn't enough for me; I wanted to make this thing work. I wanted to have the same joy the staff had. I wanted to *want* this life.

During that first month my body was recovering from fifteen years of physical abuse. The first few days I shook uncontrollably with withdrawals, and my veins pounded with pain. My body craved the chemical high that it had survived on for many years. At night I slept in fitful catnaps, still suffering from the nightmares of the past. For the first time in years I was getting three good meals a day, but my system couldn't handle the regularity. I had no strength, no endurance, and even ordinary day-to-day activity was more than I could handle. It was all I could do to walk up the two long flights of steps to the third-floor dorm, for example. But after that first month I started to feel a little better.

More important than my physical improvement was my new mental outlook: I had hope for the first time in fifteen years. I found out that Teen Challenge had been started on the streets of New York by Dave Wilkerson for addicts just like me—that hundreds of addicts' lives had been changed because of it. I'd never before met an addict who'd quit, but Teen Challenge has an 80 percent recovery rate. *It could be done.*

But it wasn't easy. One night when I couldn't sleep, I got up as quietly as I could from my bed in the twelve-bed dorm so that I wouldn't wake any of the other guys. I walked down the quiet hall to a window at the end. I sat down on the old iron radiator under the window and stared out at the lights of the city spread before me. It seemed that I was watching a stage with strangely familiar scenes. They beckoned to me, seemed to call me out. I felt as though I was the actor they were all waiting for. A strangely compelling urge to run outside came over me.

About a half-block away was the busy eight-lane Eisenhower Expressway leading to the downtown Loop. Teen Challenge is on the north side of the Eisenhower, and I had lived for part of my childhood less than a mile away, just over on the south side. I remembered times when my friends and I had played ice hockey down on the Eisenhower when it was being built. It was still called the Congress Expressway back then.

From my window on the third floor I could almost see McClaren School, the elementary school I had attended when I was a kid. And just down the street to the west was Crane Vocational High School. I'd gone there for a couple of semesters and then dropped out.

To the east I saw the downtown skyline of the Loop. I've always loved the tall, cement jungle of downtown Chicago. I heard the blaring horns, saw the flashing lights—and deep within me the music of the streets began to play the old familiar songs. In my mind I went down all the streets I'd known, passed the many lounges where I'd spent my time in years gone by. I saw the Loop with all its life before me. I knew it like the back of my hand. It was home to me; the streets of Chicago were in my blood. The excitement of nighttime in the Loop had been a part of me for many years. But never before had I felt their pull with such intensity as I did at that moment—and never since.

For a moment as I sat looking out the window I felt trapped. The stone walls of that big old run-down mansion on Ashland Avenue seemed to be keeping me away from where I longed to be.

"Man, it's time to hit the streets again!" I said softly. "I gotta get back out there where the action is."

As I sat there staring longingly out at the beckoning nighttime lights, a movement by the old shed below my window caught my eye. As I watched, the biggest rat I'd ever seen crawled out from under the shed and headed for the bags of garbage we'd set out for the garbage men to take. No, it was Tarzan! We'd named him that because of his huge size and matching meanness. He charged at anyone who came his way.

I watched as he made his nightly forage for some food. He went from sack to sack, digging furiously for any kind of crumbs that he could find. I watched him rip into a bag of spoiled food, probably green with mold, and as he gobbled up the filthy, stinking mess I felt my stomach churn inside me. For a moment I felt the old familiar physical wrenching of my insides, and I grabbed my stomach, lowered my head between my legs, and prepared to throw up.

But I didn't. I picked my head back up, and as I looked outside for Tarzan, I saw myself instead. I sat there by the window captive, bound to memories. One memory stood out clearest of all.

I remembered a cold December night when I had wandered down Skid Row, past flophouses and drunks sleeping on the curb. I was sick, tired, and too poor to pay the couple of bucks to spend the night in any of the bedbug-infested flophouses I staggered past. So I turned the corner and half-staggered, half-crawled back to the alley lot where several garbage trucks were parked overnight.

I passed a dumpster loaded with garbage. The lid was open, and even in the cold, frozen air the stench of the garbage made me heave. It didn't matter: I was too sick to search for anything to eat.

The trucks were parked just beyond. I went from truck to truck until I found one with the cab door unlocked, so that I could crawl in and get out of the forty-below winds of the night. I grabbed a stick off the ground and hit the side of the truck. Several rats crawled out the open door, jumped off, and ran away. I crawled up to the cab and climbed inside.

"Gotta get some sleep," I moaned, and as I lay my head down, the tears rolled down my face. I didn't know if the cold wind outside had caused them, or if it was the ache inside.

Sitting by that window at Teen Challenge, I felt that same ache again. I reached up to wipe the tears away. As I did so, I looked out the window from where I sat and saw Tarzan scurrying away. Suddenly he brought reality of the streets back home to me.

Hey, I thought, there's something happening to me here inside these walls of Teen Challenge that's never happened before in my life. I can see the streets for what they are. "That's death out there," I told myself. "The life is inside!"

For the first time in my life I felt really good about myself. I was with people who cared about me even though they knew the mess I'd made of my life. That caring aspect had a tremendous impact on me. Irene's peanut butter sandwich had come at a time when I had absolutely nothing to offer in return—nothing that she or any of the others there would want to con me out of. Yet they still loved me! They knew all about me—and they *still* loved me! The tears began to roll down my cheeks again as I felt the warmth of the love here at Teen Challenge. I leaned against the cold windowpane and instantly pulled back, turning my face toward the warmth I'd found inside.

I thought about the nights I'd tried to grab a few quick moments of sleep out there. I couldn't trust anyone, so I slept most nights with a hand on my knife or gun in case someone tried to sneak up on me. Or in the middle of a park under a neon light so that I could see anyone who tried to creep up on me. The memory of my night in a Salvation Army dropbox with a wino I'd never before met flashed before my eyes. That night I'd turned my back to him—something I'd never dared to do. Yet here I was now, sleeping like a baby with eleven other exaddicts.

I thought about the recent changes in me. The guilt was completely gone. All at once I saw my mother's face: "Mom, you may never forgive me for what I did to you. But Jesus has! He took my pain away. I don't see your finger pointing at me any longer. I don't have to pay the price anymore. This man Jesus did it for me. Jesus paid it all. He took my rap, and he let me go free!"

For the first time since her death I wished Mom could see me, could hear me tell her how I felt. I knew that now I could become a man that she'd be proud of. I knew I *would!* She wouldn't be ashamed of me any longer. *I* wasn't ashamed of me any longer either! And for the first time in years I remembered my mom's smile.

That night, there at that window, I knew that I'd never stare out at the streets with longing again. I wanted more of Jesus. I wanted the life I'd found inside these walls. I set my heart to learn to be the man I finally felt someone could help me to become.

I remembered what Ken had told me a couple days before: "Jim," he had said, "God's cleaned your life completely out. He's taken out all the pain, all the sin, all the garbage. From now on, whatever you put in your life, that's what you'll be. If you put bad stuff back, that's how you'll feel — bad! But if you start putting good stuff there inside, you'll feel good, you'll *be* good!"

I didn't know how to put good things in. I didn't even know what was good. I had no morals, no value system, nothing valid within myself to guide me. So I became a "watcher." I observed everybody. I wanted to see if this Jesus stuff really worked. I had to find out how to *make* it work. I wanted to see if these people were for real. I wanted to know where the cracks were in their armor. If fifteen years on the streets had taught me anything, it was to be able to quickly size people up — figure them out, find out what their game was, find out how to get at them if the need arose.

Well, I found a few cracks and saw a few inconsistencies, especially in the guys on the program. But they kept trying. And I found out something else: this Jesus stuff wasn't a game — it was a life! An experience that worked. Jesus really could take a broken, rotten addict and change that man into something good. He did it. He was the one who held me up till I could stand alone. He was the one who walked beside me all the way. When it seemed too hard, he said, "Come on, Jim — you and I together will do it!" And the life of Jesus worked twenty-four hours a day, seven days a week. It worked when you were successful, but it also worked when you failed! It worked inside you! I didn't have to play a game, figure out the moves. *God did that!*

Gradually I was learning more about the ways of God from the chapel services and from the other guys in the program. But one day Ken said, "Jim, you're going to have to read God's Word. If you don't read the Bible, you can't make it."

I tried to read the passages he suggested, but nothing seemed to make any sense to me. Man, I thought, I'm not a reader — I'm a *doer!*

But I kept trying. Finally I prayed my first request to God. I hadn't dared to ask him for anything except forgiveness up to now.

"God," I prayed, "I want this life. I want to know how to live for you. But if I gotta find out how from this book, I don't think I can do it. I don't understand a word it says! Please, you gotta help me, God!"

It felt so strange to cry for help to someone. Everything I'd learned had taught me never to depend on someone else. Or let anyone else depend on me. People who depended on others only got hurt. I'd hurt so many, and I'd been hurt. I'd depended on Dad, and he'd let me down; he wasn't there when I needed him. I depended on others, and they let me down. And I still remembered all the times I'd broken the trust of so many who cared about me. It was foreign to be dependent. Even the drugs on which I'd depended as the only thing that could help me had turned on me! Yet while it felt strange to call on this God who'd changed my life, I knew somehow that he'd never let me down!

One night right after supper I sat down on my bed to try again. In a couple hours I realized I'd read through eight chapters of Matthew with real understanding.

"God, I did it!" I prayed gratefully. "You answered my prayer—you helped me! My mind *can* understand this book." He didn't let me down then or ever. He cared enough about me to hear me when I called. I was worth his help. I could come to God on my own, tell him my needs, and get his help! I knew now that I would make it.

Most of all I watched Ken. It was obvious that he was genuinely good. But it was more than that. He was always there, always showing me that he cared about me. He didn't say that he loved me and then act as though he didn't care about me at all. He never hurt me, never let me down.

I found myself wanting to be just like him. I knew I'd make it if I could just learn how to live my life as Ken lived his. I wanted to be worthy of his trust. I wanted to be the kind of man that other people could depend on. As I depended on Ken. He was there for me—any time I needed him. I wanted to learn to be there for others. I wanted to be a part of others, of this family at Teen Challenge. I wanted to give myself away for the first time in my life.

Ken was extremely sensitive to the needs of everyone in our little household. He could anticipate what we needed most and was always there for us. He really loved us; he really wanted us to make it. His entire life was consumed with taking us from the depths of failure to the heights of victory.

One time four or five of us were sitting around on the living-room couches talking about our experiences of getting high on dope. The staff didn't want us falling into the trap of just talking about junk, but that's exactly what we were doing.

Ken came bounding upstairs from the basement. "Come on, you guys, we're going to play a game!" he said, grinning at us. I thought, Hey, Ken, split. We don't want to play no kids' game!

But he just sat there smiling, explaining how to play this silly game. He got us all in a big circle and then he stood in the center, grinning from ear to ear as he taught us the "rules." He would point to one of us and call out the name of an animal—"elephant." The two guys on either side of the one he pointed to had to make the ears on the guy in the middle, and the middle guy had to make the nose.

We really got into this game in spite of ourselves. Ken roared his deep, happy laugh, and we held our aching sides as we laughed as much at him as we did at the spectacle we were making of ourselves. Tears ran down my face, and I couldn't stop laughing. I felt light, full of joy, far removed from the junk we'd been talking about just minutes ago. We played and laughed for an hour. It was the most fun I'd had in years.

"Oh, no!" Ken suddenly exclaimed, looking at his watch. "Rowena is gonna kill me! I told her I'd be home on time for supper tonight without fail." Then, with a grin, he said, "Well, she's always accused me of loving you guys more than her." We knew he was kidding, but it sounded great—and we felt his love.

After Ken left and we were sitting there still laughing about that childish game that had made us feel like kids again. I thought, I've met a lot of sharp people in my time; I was pretty slick myself. But this Ken is the smoothest guy I've ever seen! He knows just how to maneuver us. Brother Smooth—that's Ken Schmidgall. I sat there thinking about the tremendous impact his sincere interest in me had had on my life. He really loved me, really loved all the guys.

One night Ken called, "C'mon, you guys. Let's go hit the streets again with Jesus." We grabbed our Bibles and piled into the old bus. The tires were bald, and there was no heater. The first thing we did every time we piled in was pray, "Lord, keep the bus going tonight."

Ken headed down to 42nd Street, in one of Chicago's worst neighborhoods. I was scared to death to talk to those guys about Christ.

I knew them—if not by name, at least by reputation. But Ken was smiling away, singing "Victory in Jesus" at the top of his lungs. It didn't matter to him that many of these guys carried knives and guns. Or that no one ever crossed them or confronted them without being sorry that he had. They were totally unpredictable, crazy. I'd been wary of them in my old life; I'd never come down here to cop a fix without my hand on my gun. And now Ken wanted me to tell them about Christ!?

We walked the street in pairs, talking to everyone we met about the power of God to change lives.

I walked with Ken. He stopped beside a mean-looking gang hanging out on a corner—six or eight guys standing there. They were young—in their late teens or early twenties—and had cigarettes hanging from their mouths. Most of them had on black shirts and dirty Levis. A couple of them had on leather vests.

Ken turned to two of the guys, both of them tall and tough. They made Ken look like a little kid between them. He stuck out his hand, and when they didn't respond he began talking to them. "Hey, what's happening?" he asked.

"Nothing," one of them muttered.

"Well, you ought to hear what's happened to these guys here," he went on, pointing to me and a couple of the other guys from Teen Challenge who had just walked up.

The two guys looked at us but didn't say anything.

Ken went on: "Hey, you know Jim Dycus?" he asked, pointing to me. "He just put in almost a year at Cook County Jail."

I felt like falling into a subway vent as they looked me over, but they still didn't say anything.

"Well, he's going to be telling what just happened to him," Ken said, "right over there, in that little store." He pointed to the little storefront church we planned to meet in. "Come on over and listen at seven o'clock tonight."

He began walking away, then turned around and, with a smile, called, "See you later!"

Later we met the pastor of that little nondenominational storefront church and went inside to have a testimonial meeting. Old folding chairs filled the room. There was a rickety wood pulpit up in front. The walls were painted green, and checkerboard linoleum was on the floor. By the time we got through the song part of the service, that

little church had really come alive. The thirty or so people there—
some from Teen Challenge, others drawn from the streets by the
music—were on their feet, singing at the top of their lungs, clapping
their hands, and swaying to the music. Ken was beating on a tambou-
rine he'd picked up off a chair, and we were all feeling good and free
with joy. More alive and excited in that little storefront church than
I'd ever felt in any of the so-called nightspots that I used to party in
on Rush Street, I felt an electric jolt of anticipation.

After the music a couple of the guys on the program told how God
had changed their lives. Then Ken poked me: "It's your turn, Jim," he
said.

Although I'd been out street-witnessing with Ken and the guys
several times before, tonight I would speak for the first time.

As I walked to the pulpit, the front door opened. In walked several
members of the street gang that Ken and I had encountered. They had
their black-and-red gang jackets on, and they filed in looking everyone over with those hard, cold, empty eyes I recognized so well. They
formed a line across the back of that little church and just stood there,
staring at us, arms crossed in front of them. I felt their aggressive
command of the room, and a chill ran up and down my spine. Every
instinct told me that this could be trouble. My knees weakened, and
I wanted to bolt off that little platform where I stood.

But Ken just grinned reassuringly. "Isn't this great, Jim?" he
whispered to me. "They came to hear what you have to say."

Knees shaking, I started speaking, telling how God had changed
my life. I talked about my years on drugs. It was the hardest thing I'd
ever done. I felt defenseless and naked to everyone within earshot. I
didn't know how that gang was going to react, but I knew how I
would have reacted in my old life. I remembered the young kids I'd
met in jail, and how their inexperience had made them victims of the
older, more seasoned men. I felt as vulnerable as one of them, waiting
for that gang to close in on me.

But suddenly the presence of my God was there with me. I didn't
stand alone! I knew that what he'd done for me he could do for them,
and I longed to let them know. I knew they needed him as much as
I did.

When I was done, Ken got up and told how the same God who
changed our lives could change anyone's life. That gang stood there
motionless through it all—my words and Ken's. But when Ken gave

an altar call, a couple of the leaders walked forward for prayer, and then several of the rest of them walked up and knelt in front to give their lives to God.

It was a tremendously moving experience for me. I saw the power of God transform those lives, and I recognized how great that power was. They were low-life, just as I had been. They were hard, cold, walled up inside their bondage to Satan where no one could reach them. Only the grace of God, administered through the love of God in the power of God, could zero in and grab their hearts for God. And God had used *me* to help! My life had helped someone else! I *did* have something to give! The pain that I'd experienced in my past could now be used to prove the power of God to change a life. My pain was worth it all. My past could point others to their future in Christ. I started burning with a desire to share my new life with everyone who lived in death as I had.

A few days after that I stood in the bathroom early one morning shaving. All the while I was thinking about the new life God had given me. I happened to glance at my eyes, and I was so excited by what I saw that I dropped my razor and shouted at the top of my lungs, "Ken, Ken, come and see, come and see!"

The whole household came running. For all they knew I could have just slit my wrists, I was shouting so loudly.

As Ken bounded into the bathroom, I pointed to my eyes. "Look at 'em, Ken, look at 'em!"

"Look at what, Jim?" he asked.

I grabbed him, pulled him closer, and pointed at my eyes in the mirror.

"My eyes, Ken—look at my eyes," I said, laughing with delight. "There's a twinkle in them!" God had put a sparkle in my eyes that had never been there before. No longer the windows into a dead soul, they shone with the new life God had given me. They radiated the life that I now had within me. I felt a rush of spiritual energy pass through my body that I had never felt before. Though it felt like a high, I knew that this was no temporary thing that would leave me, force me back into a living death. It was life itself—new life deep within!

I stayed at Teen Challenge nine months, and my time there was fantastic. When I left, I felt as though I'd been through spiritual boot camp. I knew that I'd been prepared to live a changed life, that I'd be able to be strong for God wherever I went from that time on. I was a brand-new man. Everything was new—most of all my new desire. Before all I ever wanted was to do drugs. Now all I wanted was to live for God. I started wondering what God wanted me to do with this new life.

After one of the chapel services with a visiting evangelist, he singled me out and talked to me. "The Lord is going to use you in the ministry in a mighty way!" he told me.

My heart jumped in my chest, and there was a lump in my throat. It was beyond my comprehension to believe that God could use me, but it was what I longed for. It was what I wanted more than anything else. But I still had trouble really believing that God wanted *me!* Who was I that God could use me? All I had to offer as credentials for service were fifteen years of heroin addiction and alcoholism, a police record a mile long, and four divorces! What kind of résumé for ministry is that?

I felt God leading me back to the Salvation Army Social Service Center to share with the guys there who knew me so well. I felt that God wanted me to make restitution for all the agony I had given them.

I went back and started sweeping the warehouse floor again. I asked the men I'd hurt to forgive me. I started telling them about the change that God had made in me. I made my stand right away, boldly telling them that God could do the same for them.

The first night I was there, and every night and morning after that, I knelt by my bed in that forty-bed dormitory and prayed for strength and guidance.

Although at first the guys called me "Holy Joe," as the months went on they gave me their respect. But I had to earn it.

One night soon after I came back, I ran down to the canteen in the television room to get a Coke. One of the guys saw me and loudly announced, "Oh, there's that Jesus freak."

I remember looking at the table where he sat. I knew it was important not to back down. But I had to stand up to them in a Christian spirit, not the way I would have in my old life.

I smiled at all of them, and said, "Yup, I sure love Jesus for what he did for me." Then I turned and went back upstairs.

My heart broke for the men there. Many of them were old buddies of mine, guys I'd shot dope with or drunk with. I longed to see a change in their lives like the one I'd experienced. It was so hard for me to know what they needed and not be able to convince them to go for it! One of them was Scotty. He looked about sixty, but he was only in his early forties.

"Hey, Holy Joe, leave me alone. I don't need your religion," he said as I helped him up to his feet from the pavement, where he'd fallen in a drunken stupor.

When I had brought him around, he begged, "If you *really* want to help, give me a dollar."

"Sorry, I can't do that, Scotty," I told him. But I took him back to the dormitory with me and talked them into letting him come back into the Salvation Army program even though he'd just walked off it. I remembered when I had done the same thing.

I pulled a bill out of my wallet. "Put this five dollars in his account," I told the desk clerk. "When Scotty sobers up, he'll need it."

When I became store supervisor for the Salvation Army, Casey worked for me. He was a big, ugly man who really looked mean. Many days he came in drunk, and I'd help him pull himself together. I cried many times for him, and as I did so the Lord revealed to me that it was only through his transforming love that I was able to shed tears for a mean old black man. Only a few months ago I would have either laughed at his plight or simply not cared. But now I could see his need, and I wanted to be able to help him. Just as Ken and Teen Challenge had helped me by pointing me to Christ.

One day Casey didn't show up for work, so I called the director at the Center. "Brigadier, Casey didn't come in today. Have you heard from him?"

"Jim, we just got word that he's been killed," the director informed me. "Apparently he got drunk and was involved in a brawl."

"Oh, God," I prayed, "why couldn't I reach him? Help me know how to reach these guys. Let me bring them to you!"

I'd never had compassion for people like this before. God was completely turning my heart around to feel something I'd never felt in my life.

I started singing in the Army choir. Every time I stood looking across the chapel filled with men who'd lost all hope, my heart burned to tell them of Christ, who could give them new life. Each time I led one of them to the Lord, I grew stronger in my desire to live for this God who had changed my hell to happiness.

But my life wasn't without struggles. Even though I had placed myself in God's hands, the devil still came around to hassle me. One of his greatest attacks came one day in the warehouse.

It was one of the days when we were unloading several truckloads of donated goods just recently picked up. I was store supervisor, and I was talking to the dock foreman about the distribution of the goods to the various stores.

"Go get Dycus. He'll know what to do with them," I heard one of the guys call.

Turning, I saw all the warehouse workers gathered in a group around one of the dumpsters. I walked over to where they stood. "What'cha got?" I asked.

One of them thrust a box in my hands. I looked down at a brand-new box of fifty disposable syringes! My mind raced. There was a time I would have done anything to hold just *one* syringe. Here in my hands I held *fifty.* Fifty highs — fifty chances to feel that rush again.

"Guys, I know exactly what to do with these!" I said. I knew that they were testing me; that's why they'd called me over. I raised that box of needles high above my head and began to walk away. As I walked, I thought about the times in my past when I'd craved a fix but had no needle to stick in my arm. My veins burned, and the old cravings flooded back. It was only through the superhuman strength of God that I could hold that box above my head.

"I can do anything through God's strength," I said softly, praying as I walked, "God, make me strong — keep my arms up!"

I hurried to the door and out to the warehouse platform. When I reached the edge of the platform I threw that box into the dumpster and slammed the lid shut. The moment that box left my hand the cravings ceased. The presence of God filled my life instead.

"That's where junk belongs!" I shouted to the guys who stood there watching. "I don't need it anymore. I don't need that rush. I'm clean, free, brand-new inside. All I need is my God!"

15. Fantasy to Family

A few months later Ellen Birch, my "spiritual mom," and I were riding along the street on our bikes. I had met Ellen before my conversion in the alcoholic treatment program at Lutheran General Hospital in Park Ridge, near Chicago; she had been a nurse assigned to my ward. I had thought she was a "religious fanatic" at the time and enjoyed trying to give her a hard time. But nothing I did seemed to ruffle her gentle spirit. She seemed to really care about me. She had a warm, loving spirit and a smile that was genuine.

I hadn't let her inside my defensive walls at the hospital. But we had met again months later at Teen Challenge. Ellen and her husband, Ed, often visited the guys at the Center, and they had become true, loving friends of mine.

"God has really blessed me," I remarked to her as we pedaled along the streets of Winnetka, where Ed and Ellen lived.

"You're growing so fast in your faith, Jim," she replied.

"Well, I think it's time to take another step of faith," I said.

"What do you mean?" she asked.

"I think it's time I started praying for a wife!"

I don't remember her answer, but she probably was as doubtful about my ability to be a husband as the disciples were about the woman at the well of Samaria. After all, I'd loused up my relationships as much as the woman of Samaria had.

Nevertheless, I felt God's approval of my prayer request. So I began to pray, "Lord, send me a wife with the look of Jesus on her face."

Having a real family had been a fantasy of mine for years. My eyes filled with tears and an ache arose deep inside me each time I remembered lonely Christmas seasons in the Loop of Chicago. When I saw happy families walking hand in hand along the lighted streets, I would stand on a busy corner in the Loop imagining that I was among them with my wife and children. I would close my eyes, and as I did so I would feel the touch of my imagined family's hands, hear their voices commenting on the sights in festive store windows that we passed. Those dreams were always shattered by the return of reality. I no longer had a family — only broken dreams. When I got saved, I had faced the issue of the family I had lost. I had resolved in my heart that I'd probably never try to see Connie again. I knew the terror that my reentering her life would bring.

But a couple of times I parked my car down the street from where she lived. The tears flowed from my eyes as I sat there hoping to catch a glimpse of my girls. I didn't know what would happen if Connie saw me. Probably she'd call the cops to come and take me away again.

I knew the most honorable thing that I could do for Connie was to leave her alone. I vowed never to cause her pain again. I wanted her to be happy!

One night I walked into the Salvation Army Belmont Corps for Sunday evening worship. (A Salvation Army Corps is like a church.) As I sat down, I heard the officer in charge announce, "Tonight Captain Barbara Cramer will be speaking to us."

"Great, a lady preacher!" I whispered sarcastically to my friend Jake beside me. I watched her face as she spoke on "Spiritual Surgery," and suddenly I remembered my prayer request: "Lord, let me see the love of Jesus on her face." I realized that that was what I was seeing on this Salvation Army captain's face. She had a beautiful smile that radiated Jesus.

A couple of weeks later she was in the congregation when I shared how God had transformed my life. For the first time she heard about the kind of life I'd lived. "It's hard to believe you were ever the guy you talked about that night," she told me later.

We both attended that same corps regularly, and soon her group of friends and several of us younger guys from the Social Service Center had become friends. We began to socialize together. We bowled together or would go as a group to a movie and then out for a snack afterward. I admired Barb's friendliness, as well as her dedication to her full-time ministry work with the Salvation Army. I had heard that she was going with a Salvation Army captain in the South, but she was always friendly and open to me.

Barb told me later that she and her friends were busy planning my future. "Jim Dycus is really a great guy," Barb told them. "We ought to get him and Laura together. They'd make a great couple! Next time we all go bowling together, let's put Jim and Laura on the same lane, and before the night is over he'll ask her out."

Their plan worked almost perfectly. All of us had a great time together that night.

"Let's go across the street for pizza," I suggested. As we left the bowling alley, I managed to walk next to Barb.

"Ginny and Dan are going out for tacos next Sunday night after church," I mentioned to her. "How would you like to come along with me?"

She looked at me in consternation. "You're supposed to ask *Laura* out tonight!" she managed to answer. But she went with me.

After that first double-date with our friends, Barb and I began to date steadily. It was months before we talked about our love, but we both knew from the start that God was doing something special in our relationship.

We came from vastly different backgrounds. Barb came from a conservative Christian background. She had never smoked a cigarette, didn't know the taste of booze, and had never lost her purity to a man. Her greatest sin had been stealing watermelons back in Michigan as a teen. She'd always assumed that God would send her a twentieth-century version of Daniel or Martin Luther for a mate. What a dilemma to discover *me*!

The more we got to know each other, the more aware she became that there were really two Jim Dycuses: the broken, defeated, hopeless addict that I used to be, and the fully forgiven, reconstructed new creature in Christ that I am today. One night while attending a conference in Los Angeles, she asked God what to do about my past. She felt in her heart that she had two choices: she could indulge in curiosity about my old life, ask hundreds of questions about the past, or she could do as God had already done with my past—forget it and never let it become an obstacle to our developing relationship. She chose the latter. And because she did, willingly believing in my less-than-year-old faith in God, I was able to begin learning to trust myself. Her gift of trust put legs on my faith, and through the power of the Holy Spirit and Barb's trust I no longer was afraid to walk away from my past. I was free to live fully in the bright and hopeful new future that God had given me.

God had done so much for me. I was living at the Men's Social Service Center. I still didn't have much of anything to call my own. I'd arrived there with the clothes on my back, a toothbrush from the county jail, three pennies from my old life, the medal I wore around my neck, and my Bible. It was such a contrast to the man I used to be. That man had needed money and material possessions to feel secure. But the new man God was creating in me no longer needed worldly goods to feel secure. All I wanted was the spiritual riches of my forgiven life. All I longed for was to serve this God who loved me. *God loved me!* And now, so did Barb!

One morning I walked down the hall to the shower singing at the top of my lungs, "I'll fly away, O Glory, I'll fly away . . ."

From one of the other rooms I heard a booming voice: "I wish you would!"

But even that jolt back into reality couldn't dampen my joy. God had healed me totally from the crippling memories of my broken past. In place of pain there was a joy that never went away, and a thirst to become the someone I could never be without him.

But learning to express that joy to Barb was another matter. What did I know about dating a pure girl? Barb was the first woman I'd been with since years before. I hadn't cared about women much during my last years as an addict, and I had hardly even looked at them since my conversion. I didn't much want to be around them. To me they represented flesh and failure. I had never had a good, fulfilling relationship with any woman—let alone a Christian woman. I kept them at a distance, always giving myself space to walk away to ward off being hurt. But Barb was already inside those walls, and I wanted to keep her there. Yet what did I know about establishing a godly relationship with her?

I knew my limitations. My policy was strictly "Look but do not touch." I didn't even shake her hand! My lack of emotional expression confused her. Even though I was feeling many emotions that I hadn't experienced in years, and some that I'd never experienced, telling her about them was still too hard for me to do. I hadn't told her of my limitations, so she didn't know what the problem was.

On our eleventh date, I took her to the Museum of Science and Industry. Because it was free, it was one of the few places we could afford! I could tell that she was bothered about something. Finally she grabbed my hand and said, "If you want me to walk through here with you, you're going to have to hold my hand." I didn't let go for several hours!

Because Barb was still a commissioned Salvation Army officer, we tried to keep the news of our developing relationship quiet. She would be required to resign her commission if we should decide to marry: a Salvation Army officer can marry only another Salvation Army officer. We were not ready to deal with those consequences yet.

Many of our dates consisted of my going over to her apartment for a homecooked meal—many times with one or two of my friends from the Center. Barb never knew whether I'd arrive alone or with someone in tow. Thanksgiving was one of those times.

"Hey, Jim, where you going for Thanksgiving?" my friend Ben asked. He already knew, and I guessed why he was asking.

"Over to Barb's. Want to come along?" I answered.

"Man, I'd love to," he quickly replied. "Do you think she'd care?"

"Of course not!"

"Well, do you think it would be all right if Langley came along too?" He lived at the Center also.

Laughing, I said, "Sure, meet you by my car at eleven-thirty."

So on Thanksgiving morning we met. I climbed into the driver's side of my car—an old Rambler that Ed and Ellen Birch had given me—and Langley climbed in back. Ben was sliding into the front seat when I saw Charles Allen heading our way.

"Close the door, Ben," I prompted and quickly made a U-turn. Rolling down the window, I waved at Charles and called. "See you later." I made myself ignore the disappointment on his face, because I knew that two extras were enough. Besides, I didn't want to have to share too much of dinner!

Barb had been busy cooking all morning. As she greeted us at the door, the smell of dinner welcomed us inside. I glanced over at the table. There were four place settings! "Hey," I whispered to her, "how did you know there would be four of us?"

With a look of mock disgust she whispered back, "Guess I'm getting to know you!"

Thanksgiving with Barb that first year was full of promise. Every holiday in the past had been empty, wasted. But now God had begun to let me realize my hopes, to live in real happiness, instead of only dreaming about it.

As Christmas approached we grew much closer. I felt the joy of knowing that someone trusted me, someone cared for me again. I knew what it felt like to love again, to share myself, my hopes and dreams, and to feel that love returned. A few days before Christmas we went out together and bought a real Christmas tree and brought it back to her apartment to decorate. As I carried the tree into her building, I remembered the first Christmas I spent in jail. I remembered the ride home with Dad on January 11, and the welcoming sight of the lights of the Christmas tree Mom had left up until I came home.

As I walked in the door to Barb's apartment, I thought about the longing I'd had that Christmas long ago to see my mother. I glanced toward Barb's kitchen, half-expecting to see Mom. But she wasn't there! And like a bad dream that you can remember but no longer have, the memory of Mom's finger pointing at me rushed over me and I thought about her words: "Jimmy, someday you'll be sorry for all you've done!" The memory was still there, but it no longer hurt; the sting of pain was gone!

I was moved with emotion as we trimmed the tree, then sat back to admire our work. Christmas had always represented pain and loneliness. But sitting there with Barb, I was completely filled with overwhelming joy.

And this year I was to have a real *family* Christmas. In the middle of December Barb had invited me to travel with her to Michigan to meet her parents, and to spend Christmas with her sister's family. I hadn't been sure just what to do. "Dear God," I'd prayed, "for so many years I've had only broken dreams and painful memories about a family. But now it seems as though you've given me new hope. I love Barb, and she's willing to introduce me to her family. But what if they can't accept me?"

I tried to look at me from their viewpoint. Barb had already told her parents a little about me, I knew. Their reaction had been guarded apprehension. Her mom and dad were very proud of Barb's full-time ministry, and they knew that her relationship with me could end all that.

But there was an even bigger reason why they didn't want her to be involved with me. "My parents are worried because you've been divorced," Barb told me. "They don't want me involved with a divorced man."

She went on to tell me why. Her parents had been solid Christians most of their lives, active in a church that didn't believe in divorce. Then in 1959 their own marriage had crumbled; they had divorced. The church had asked them to leave, and very few of their church friends had maintained any contact with them. They had been so traumatized by the event that they had never found recovery from their guilt and pain. They couldn't bear the thought of their own daughter going through a similar experience because of her relationship with a divorced man. "But don't worry," Barb assured me, "once they get to know you they'll love you as much as I do!"

Christmas that year was like a dream come true for me. Barb's sister had the biggest tree I'd ever seen. Both her parents were there. The presents rose up three feet from the floor. Christmas dinner was a feast such as I'd never experienced. When I thought I'd burst, her mom reminded me, "Don't forget to save room for dessert!"

After dinner we opened gifts. The house was filled with family and friends, and everyone received about a dozen presents. And every family member there had purchased one for me! I learned later that Barb had sent a carefully detailed list of things I wanted and needed, with instructions that every item be ready for me. It was the first Christmas since my childhood that the holiday was "right"!

On the flight home I asked, "How do you think they liked me?"

She smiled and answered, "Well, Dad told me it looked as if there was something to you, but that I should take it slow and let you prove yourself."

"That's all?" I asked.

"No," she continued. "He also told me I was big enough to make my own decisions!"

Suddenly I liked her dad a lot more for his wisdom! After that first Christmas in Michigan one thing seemed certain to me: I knew that Barb was the answer to my prayer for a wife. I knew that God had brought us together. God had called me into full-time ministry, and Barb was already there. I was in love, happy—and scared to death!

I was fearful of letting my feelings out, of expressing them to Barb. Here I was, a street-wise, former man-about-town with a past filled with scores of women, a pimp of the past, divorced four times, and yet I was so paranoid that I was afraid to hold Barb's hand or kiss her!

Finally it got so hard on Barb that I had to take her to Ken for counseling. I took *her*, but he straightened *me* out! With his help I was able to talk about my feelings—and fears—and we began to work together to communicate our fears as well as share our joys. Our relationship grew even stronger, and I eventually discovered that I was ready to make a permanent commitment to Barb.

January 21, 1973, arrived—the one-year anniversary of my new life in Christ. My first birthday! Barb and I spent the day together and in the evening sat down on the couch to listen to music. As we sat there, arms around each other, listening to "Because He Lives," I thought my heart would burst it was so full of happiness. Because of Christ, and all he'd done for me, I lived, and the life that he had given me was filled with promise.

We sat quietly on the couch for many minutes after the record ended. But while I was quiet on the outside, within I was bursting to speak. Finally I managed to ask, "How would you like to spend the rest of your life with me?"

Without a moment's hesitation Barb replied, "I'd *love* to!"

It was done. My prayer was answered. I'd never have to stand alone at Christmas time watching happy families in the Loop again. I'd never watch mothers hurry their children across the street to avoid contact with me again. And I'd never wake up from my fantasy family to the rude reality of isolation and pain again. God had given me my own family.

I remembered my prayer that night one year ago in the chapel of Teen Challenge. "If you'll make me happy like these others, I'll do anything you want me to do, I'll be anything you want me to be, and I'll go anywhere you want me to go."

In just one short year God had fulfilled his side of that promise far beyond my wildest expectations! But while the joy that Barb and I shared was unequaled by anything I'd ever known, the immediate future proved to be somewhat less appealing.

Barb and I decided that we would marry on June 2, 1973, less than six short months away. We discovered that we couldn't put off any longer facing the consequences of letting the Army know of our decision.

That next week she went to her supervisor and told him of our plans. His response was downright disheartening: "Barb, quite frankly I'd hoped that you'd never get to this point with Jim," he told her. "You'd better take a little time and carefully think about what you're doing!"

"I don't need to, Major," she replied. "Jim and I are sure that this is God's will for our lives."

"It will never be God's will!" he answered.

From that first encounter, Barb faced many more such confrontations. I felt helpless as she told me of the continuing persuasion tactics that the Army used to try to help her "come to her senses."

One day she sat down in her office with her secretary. This mature

Christian woman had been a wise and sympathetic support throughout, and she recognized the growing discontent Barb felt about her role. "You know, Barb, you can serve the Lord *outside* the Army just as well, and maybe better!" she counseled now.

Barb didn't answer, but suddenly she knew that God's plan for her life would be bigger than anything she'd anticipated up to now. Three weeks before our wedding, her resignation from officership became effective.

The day of the wedding everything that could go wrong did. I was so nervous and fearful that morning that I washed my clothes five or six times. Even though I'd already made a permanent commitment to Barb in my heart, the anxiety of wondering if I could *live* that commitment paralyzed me. Finally I fell to my knees beside my bed. "God, I turned my life over to you," I prayed, "and you made me who I am today. Now give me faith to believe that I can be who you want me to be in my marriage to Barb. Let me become the man you want me to be tomorrow!" I arose in confidence and left for the church.

The flowers were delivered to the wrong address. The cake fell when the bakery attempted to carry it down the basement stairs. The beautician had double-booked the wedding-morning appointments for Barb and her sister, mother, and niece. Barb's dad got lost on the way to the church, making the ceremony several minutes late. Barb herself was on the verge of tears. "Hey, if he doesn't get here soon, we'll just elope," I joked. But finally he arrived, and the ceremony began.

Right in the middle of the opening solo, a garbage truck arrived in the alley below the open sanctuary windows. As Barb's boss stepped to the window to lower it quietly, the entire pane smashed to the floor. It seemed as though the Army had been right! God must be trying to tell us that we shouldn't marry.

But as Ken began to pray the closing prayer after we had shared our vows, the Spirit of the Lord invaded that altar and wrapped us both in the assurance of God's love and blessing on our life. We rose from that altar as Mr. and Mrs. James Dycus, united by God and blessed by his sweet spirit. We were gloriously confident of a beautiful beginning in his will.

The short ride to the motel thirty miles away where we were to spend the first night of our two-night honeymoon seemed to take forever. At last I could put my arms around Barb without feeling as though I was stepping out of line. When I finally held her close, it seemed as though all my broken dreams were wiped away.

I knew joy and happiness far greater than anything I'd ever hoped to know.

16. Remember Our Deal

But even joy like that I felt on our wedding day can have its time of adjustment. Waking up the first morning with Barb beside me, I was scared to death!

"Well, I'm married—again!" I thought. Then the panic hit me: "*Now* what do I do?"

Even though I loved Barb, I'd been afraid of this morning since the night I proposed to her.

I remembered the weeks before our wedding, when I had thought about this day many times. "How will I feel when I'm married to her?" I had asked myself. Many times I'd gotten on my knees and prayed, "God, help me make this work. I love Barb and I want a life with her, but I'm scared to death that I can't make it work." I knew that in the past I'd never been able to commit myself to just one woman. It had always seemed that once the challenge was over and I'd gotten what I wanted, it was time to move on to someone new. That was my track record: I'd been unfaithful to every woman I had ever known.

"God, you promised you could change me," I prayed that morning. "You've completely changed me in so many ways. Please make me totally new in this area too. Let me be the kind of husband I know you want me to be."

Just then I looked over at the motel table where I'd dropped my ring of keys the night before. In my old life I couldn't hang onto even one key. But God had changed my life so much that now I carried keys to all the Salvation Army secondhand stores in the central region of Chicago. My boss trusted me with them.

Quietly I slid out of bed and dangled those keys in my hand. Then I prayed, "God, if I can hang onto these keys, be trusted with the responsibility that they represent, then by your grace I can hang onto this new marriage that you've given me. I *will* be the man you want me to be!"

But I was still scared. Here I was, all alone, saved only a year and a half, and beginning a marriage relationship with a woman I loved.

And she, and God, expected me to be the spiritual head of our home. If I ever needed godly counsel it's now, I thought.

It was Sunday morning and I thought about our church back home in Chicago. Although it was only thirty miles away, it seemed a thousand. When Barb got up I suggested, "How about going home to Belmont for morning worship?"

But Barb had no intention of going to her home church on her honeymoon. I tried Plan B. "Well, we're already in Joliet. Let's drive on over to Naperville and visit Ken and Rowena at their church," I said. We did, and it felt wonderful to spend the first day of our life together in church with my spiritual father, Ken.

When we went out to lunch together after the service, Ken asked where we had spent the night. When I told him he began to laugh.

"Well, Jim, it sounds as if you're going to be all right," he teased. "You and Barb stayed in the same motel, and in the same room of the motel, that Rowena and I did on our wedding night!"

Those first two or three years we spent together were full of adjustments of every sort. I'd never shared my life with anyone like this before. We were two vastly different people, and learning to live in unity had its ups and downs.

One of my biggest problems was learning to sleep so close to another person. For the last few years of my old life I had lived in isolation and fear. I had slept in open parks and under neon lights, in order to be aware of anyone coming close to me; or I had slept fitfully on little cots, rolling and tossing as memories and painful guilt disturbed my sleep.

Resting quietly with someone snuggling close was therefore not an easy task. Several times I instinctively reached out to push Barb back as I felt her lying next to me. Once or twice I actually struck out at her before I realized who she was.

Allowing her to get inside my wall of self-protection was another challenge. This being in love made me painfully vulnerable to her, and that was a feeling that I had to learn to accept. However, with each new day I discovered that I could trust Barb, let her really know me without danger that she would betray me.

Commitment was becoming a way of life for me. I desired to be committed to Barb, and I was. I didn't have to struggle with it—I just did it. God *had* made me new!

I knew that those years were preparing me to do the work my God had called me to. I began to sense with great anticipation that he had a greater purpose for my life than I could even imagine. I knew beyond a shadow of a doubt that God had put a full-time call to ministry on my life.

From the day I accepted him, all I wanted to do was serve him. I spent all the time that I could trying to become the man he had saved me to become. Barb never doubted my commitment and never questioned my faith. From the day we married she encouraged me to assume the role of spiritual leader in our home.

But although she was willing to let me be the spiritual leader, she expected me to do all the work necessary to become that leader.

"Hey, Barb, where's Zephaniah?" I asked one day.

"In the Bible," she quickly responded.

When confronted with a verse I didn't understand, I'd say, "What does this verse mean?"

Her only answer: "Use your concordance and look it up."

One of her first presents to me was a Thompson Chain Reference Bible. She taught me how to use it, then left me struggling to find answers by myself. "Do you know how hard it is for me to understand all this stuff?" I blurted out many times in frustration.

"Maybe you could find the time to enroll in some night courses down at Moody Bible Institute," she suggested.

That made me mad. She knew that I'd never even graduated from high school. It was she who had struggled with me, coaching me through weeks of preparation just to pass my GED exam. She'd heard me try to read aloud, seen me struggling to understand the simplest things. Maybe college had worked for her, but how could she expect me to make a fool of myself in front of others half my age in a class?

But I went. I signed up for Acts, Homiletics, Creative Methods of Teaching, and Piano. I dropped the piano course after the first week; I didn't have enough faith to get my fingers moving. But at the end of that first semester I brought my report card home and proudly handed it to Barb. There were two things written on the paper. "Taken for audit only" was the first thing. Under that it read, "Final grade in each course—A!"

She looked at the report card and then at me. I could tell how pleased she was, but all she said was, "You didn't expect A + 's did you?" Then, reaching over, she hugged me and said, "I *knew* you could do it."

She did, too. There were many times in those first couple of years when I probably would have given up in frustration had it not been for Barb's quiet, constant belief in me. She expected great things of me, and every time I was tempted to plateau out she encouraged me a little harder, until I once again took up the fight for excellence in my spiritual growth.

All the time she was encouraging me to develop in my spiritual intellect, I was encouraging her to open up her life to experience the fullness of the work of the Holy Spirit.

"I can't deny that I don't have the kind of faith you do," she said often. "I've been a Christian all my life, been in full-time ministry, and yet I know nothing of the level of commitment and power that you have in your two-year-old spiritual life."

Barb had been taught that the experience of baptism in the Holy Spirit and speaking in tongues was only an emotional excess. But she had witnessed firsthand this experience in my life. She had seen — and continued to see — the power of the Holy Spirit at work. She began praying for the experience for herself, and on January 7, 1975, it became a reality for her.

Step by step God was continuing our preparation. But I still felt paralyzed by my past. The guilt was gone, but the metamorphosis was not complete. The transformation was taking place, but from my personal perspective the view of what I used to be clouded my vision of the man I could become.

Part of the reason I was still so aware of my past was that in at least one area I was continually disobedient to God, and I knew it! I was still bound to a habit, and this bondage was the hardest to free myself from of any that I had ever had. I had been able, with God's help, to give up my addictions to drugs and alcohol virtually overnight. Though I struggled both physically and mentally for a period of weeks, I had never once shoved another needle into my arm or broken open another bottle of booze from the time I knelt on that chapel floor and invited Christ to be my Savior. But I had deliberately and belligerently hung onto my habit of smoking cigarettes.

I had become paranoid about my smoking. I feared that someone would see me; I worried that our church would find out. I was so wracked with guilt that I couldn't even talk about it with Barb. I knew that she hated my smoking. She had told me, "I almost refused to date you anymore when I found out that you smoked." Now I never smoked in front of her. In fact, I'd leave the apartment and drive around the block to smoke, then hurry to the bathroom when I came back to brush my teeth and rid my mouth of the smell of smoke with mouthwash. Then I'd pop a cinnamon candy into my mouth before I went out to talk with Barb.

Smoking became the devil's greatest stand in the battle over my soul. I reached the point where I knew that my decision about smoking would determine my spiritual future.

One morning after a drive around the block to smoke I sat down at the kitchen table for my morning cup of coffee. Barb was busy preparing breakfast at the counter beside me.

Suddenly a voice pierced the stillness: "Remember our deal!" I felt a shock hit me like an electric current the instant I heard it. The voice was like nothing I'd ever heard before — clear, piercing, condemning, and yet compassionate and filled with love.

I stood to my feet, looked at Barb, and asked, "Did you hear that?"

"Hear what? No, I didn't hear a thing," she answered.

Immediately I knew who it was who had spoken to me. When I knelt on that chapel floor at Teen Challenge all those months ago, I had made a deal with God: "You make me happy, like these others here, and I'll do anything you want me to do, I'll be anything you want me to be, and I'll go anywhere you want me to go," I had promised God.

Well, he had kept his part of the deal, but I hadn't kept mine. Now he was confronting me, demanding my obedience.

I ran down the two flights of steps to the parking lot outside our apartment. I unlocked and opened the car door, reached under the seat for my pack of cigarettes, and smashed them underfoot. Then I threw them in the garbage gondola beside the apartment wall and slammed the cover down with a thud.

"I'll never smoke another cigarette again," I said as I came back in the door. As I explained to Barb what had happened, the truth of my words brought a release from bondage like the release I'd experienced when I knew I'd never need another shot of heroin, never again have to bomb my brains with booze. I felt cleansed, free from guilt, and able at last to begin to shut all the doors to my past. Now I could fully turn to the future God had planned for me and press toward the mark of becoming the man he intended me to be. At that moment I was free — totally and gloriously free from bondage of any form, free to place my total dependence on the Lord, who had broken the chains of sin for me.

One other major area in which I needed his help in those early years was my search for a job that would provide adequately for a family. Since we began talking about marriage, we talked about having a family, but knew it probably wouldn't be possible for quite a while. I couldn't earn enough at the Salvation Army, so I began the search for a better-paying job. I started answering ads in the employment section of the newspaper first.

Each interview seemed to be the same as the last one. "I think there's a good chance we can use you," the interviewer would tell me, "but you'll have to complete this job application first."

My heart sank the moment I heard those words, because I knew what would follow. I had filled out many job applications, and they all asked the same two questions: "Have you ever been arrested on a felony charge?" and "Are you now, or have you ever been, addicted to narcotics?"

By the time I finished answering those two questions, the interviewer's tone had always changed. "I'm sorry, Mr. Dycus, but we don't have a position for you right now. Don't call us; we'll call you!"

I became very discouraged. "I'm never going to be anything but a Salvation Army remake!" I cried to Barb.

"Wait a minute, sweetheart," she consoled me. "Who is it who remade you?"

Immediately her words reminded me of the God who had performed the miracle of transformation in my life.

"You're right," I told her. "He must be about to give me a job beyond my wildest dreams." Sure enough, he had a plan for me. It unfolded with the help of Tony and Angela, good friends of ours from church.

They were a wonderful, vibrant Italian couple with five boisterous, energetic kids. We spent many happy evenings sitting in their kitchen eating Angela's homemade spaghetti. Being in their home was like being in a train station. You never knew if there were going to be two or twenty people grabbing meatballs from the bottomless pot of sauce always simmering on the stove.

One day as we sat in their kitchen, Tony said, "I've talked to my boss, Jim. He's looking for a warehouseman. He said for you to come in and he'd talk to you about the job."

"Thanks a lot, Tony," I said, "but I already know what he's going to say."

"What kind of faith is that?" Angela chided.

So I went in for the interview. The boss was very encouraging, very friendly. He described the job and assured me that if I got it, I'd be hired at the Teamster union payscale. That would be more than four times what I was making at the Army! Within a few weeks I could join the union, and from then on I'd receive not only union wages but union benefits as well.

It sounded too good to be true. "Don't I need to fill out a job application first?" I asked.

"Nah," he answered. "If Tony says you're a reliable worker, his word is good enough for me."

The job was mine. The Lord had seen our need and provided for that need more abundantly than I had expected. And just in time. Now, in God's perfect time, we were about to start our family. It was with great joy and anticipation that we spent Christmas with Barb's family in Michigan.

"Well, next year you'll have to add a few more presents," I teased Beth, Barb's sister.

"Why, don't you think you're getting enough?" she teased back.

"Well, there's nothing here for a baby!" I announced to everyone.

But God had other plans. One cold, bleak night in late January Barb miscarried. It seemed that our hopes of having our own family were still just that—only hopes. I held Barb as she sobbed. I had no words to comfort her, so I just cried with her, "Oh, God, help us."

As I left Barb at the hospital that night, my heart was crushed. Driving home alone to our apartment, the streetlights reminded me of the dreams for a family that the lights in the Loop had awakened in me each Christmas. For so many years I'd watched families shopping in the busy Loop and wished for a family of my own. Since my marriage to Barb, my specific prayer had been, "God, I want a son of my own, one just like me!" When Barb had told me that we were expecting, I'd rejoiced, believing that my son was on the way.

When I got home I fell on my knees beside our bed and sobbed. For the first time in my new life I felt that God wasn't answering my prayers. It was the first setback I had had, and I couldn't understand it.

I was terribly concerned for Barb. When I walked out of her hospital room, she'd been deeply dejected and disappointed. I'd never seen her that way. I realized for the first time how much she needed me, depended on me. And I didn't know how to help.

"God," I cried out, "what are you doing? Why have you allowed this thing to happen to us?"

I stayed there on my knees almost all night. And in my grief and pain God came and ministered to me. He restored my hope and made me believe again that he would one day answer my prayer for a son. "Just depend on me," he whispered quietly to my grieving heart. "I'll take care of you and Barb."

But the next morning I knew that I had to face Barb, had to find a way to encourage her, restore her hope for a child. As I drove to the hospital, I prayed for wisdom to know just what to do.

When I looked into Barb's room, I was unprepared for what I saw. Barb was sitting up, her Bible open before her on the bed. On her face was the smile I'd seen the first time that I saw her. The love of God was reflected all over her face.

"God did it, Jim," she said. "Last night as I prayed, God told me not to fear, not to sorrow, that he would give us the family that we both desire so much." Again I held her, but this time we could praise the Lord for his special comfort to us both.

Even another miscarriage later that same year didn't destroy our hope. And in October of 1978, our hope became reality. Jimmy, our firstborn son, was born, weighing in at twelve pounds.

"Well, Barb, God repaid us for both the ones we lost. Jimmy's the size of *two* babies," I joked as I held my son in the bonding room at the hospital.

As I looked down at my Jimmy, I remembered years ago hearing Mom say to me, "Your dad's so proud of you, Jimmy. You're just what he wanted; you're just like him."

Standing there in that bonding room with my own Jimmy in my arms, I made a vow to God:

"God, I promised you when you saved me that if you'd make me happy, I'd serve you all my life. You've made me happier than I ever dreamed possible. You've given me the son I always wanted. Now, God, I promise you that with your help I'll raise my son to serve you. I'll be a godly father, as much like you as I can be. Then Jimmy will see you in me. I'll be just like you so that he can be just like me — and you!"

Jackie followed in 1981. Then, when we thought our family was complete, God surprised us with Dinah in 1984.

During those years of becoming a family and being prepared for service to God, one "family" member was taken from me. In September of 1981, my spiritual father, Ken Schmidgall, went home to be with Jesus.

Barb and I drove down to Jerseyville, Illinois, where he was pastoring a church, to see him just before he died. Even then, terminally ill with cancer, he was still giving much of himself to those around him. Many people came to see him, hoping to encourage him, and left amazed because he had ministered so powerfully to them. Those few days we spent together were wonderful. I sat by his bed for hours at a stretch and listened as he encouraged me to be all that God would make me.

"Jim, I'm so proud of the man you've become," he told me. "You don't need me any longer. You're grown up in Christ. All you need is your total dependence on him."

He took out a little book and showed me the cover. "You know what this is, Jim?" he asked. "These are my love thoughts to God. Do you realize how good he's been to me? Do you know how much he loves me? How much he loves you, Jim? Give him everything you've got. Serve him every moment of your life, with every breath you have. He'll bless your life even more than he's blessed mine."

As Ken talked, I thought about the years that I had known him. I knew that his life was impeccable, so I didn't understand why God was letting this happen. But I didn't *need* to understand. I didn't doubt for a moment that God was wrapping his great big arms around Ken and carrying him through these last days.

I thought, If I were God, and if I lived up in heaven, I know who I'd want with me. The first person that I'd call to be with me would be Ken Schmidgall.

I didn't want to lose Ken. I wasn't sure I could stand alone without him to lean on. But when I attended his memorial service, God confirmed Ken's words to me.

"God, you are all in all to me," I prayed. "My life belongs to you completely. You are able to keep me victorious in you."

17. Get Me In or Get Me Out!

One night I went street-witnessing with Teen Challenge in the area around Broadway and Irving Park. As I walked down the street telling people about Jesus Christ and how he could change their lives, I passed a hotel that I remembered from my old life. A friend named Big Jim had lived there. He and I had spent almost a year together in a cell at Cook County Jail. The other inmates had labeled him Big Jim and me Little Jim. When he got out, he had moved into a room at this hotel. When I got out a bit later, I had come to see him several times, to cop a fix from him or shoot dope with him. We were both in the depths of despair in those days, and we knew it. It was the pits.

As I relived those terrible memories, I wondered whether Big Jim still lived there. Last I heard, he did. I felt that the Lord wanted me to go up and witness to him now. I knew that God could change his life as he had mine. But I wasn't so sure he'd want to hear about Jesus from me. I was even afraid of what he might do to me. I'd seen him violent before. So I didn't find out if he was still there and go up to his room. I felt miserable about it all night.

The next night we went back to the same area for more street-witnessing. I knew God had wanted me to go up to Jim's room the night before, and I had felt terrible all day because I felt like I'd let God down. I hadn't gone.

"Tonight I'm going up!" I said to myself. I walked into the lobby and spoke to the desk clerk.

"Big Jim still live in Room 42?" I asked.

The clerk looked at me closely. "Well, he did until last night," he answered.

"Where'd he go?" I asked.

"Man, the cops raided us last night," he said. Big Jim got caught in the crossfire and he's dead!"

I felt as though I'd been the one to pull the trigger! "God, I failed you miserably," I cried out, begging for forgiveness. "You told me to go up to his room and I didn't. I didn't do it, and it probably cost Jim his life."

I determined at that moment that I would never again refuse to follow the Lord's direction. I would never again contribute to another soul's going to hell simply because I was unwilling to confront that person with the life-changing power of God.

Barb and I had been attending the Salvation Army on Sunday mornings and for midweek chapel services. I was directing the choir, and we were actively involved in ministry there. We even sang duets together for the men. They begged us to sing, told us how wonderful we sounded. It wasn't until we made a tape to send to Barb's mom that we realized just how terrible our singing was! That was the last time we sang together.

But we had been spending as much time as we could at Belmont Evangelical Church on the Northwest Side of Chicago. The power of the Holy Spirit was alive there, and we needed that life to inspire and lift us. Belmont was the church that Ken had brought us to while I was still at Teen Challenge. The people there had welcomed us with open arms, and their lives had been a tremendous witness to me of the sustaining power of Christ. It was an old Italian church, and many of the people had been saints of God for many, many years.

One of those saints, the "Hallelujah Lady," had personally encouraged me to live for God many times. I had nicknamed her that because of her way of praising Jesus by calling out "Hallelujah" over and over again as the pastor preached. She looked and acted as if she'd grown up in church, but she told me how God had delivered her from a life of sin also. She said she used to drink and dance in the nightspots all the time. As I watched her praising Jesus with her arms lifted, swaying to the worship music, I couldn't imagine her in that other life. "Thank you, God," I'd whisper in prayer. "If she can live a life so transformed by your power that no one sees a shred of evidence of her life of sin, then so can I." She was like my own personal cheerleader. She always told me, "Jim, God is going to use you in a mighty way — just give him everything you've got."

Soon we felt that we should make the spiritual break from the Salvation Army and make Belmont Evangelical Church our home. We notified the Army director and became members at Belmont, an Assemblies of God church.

One day the pastor called us into his office. "Jim, I want you to consider teaching the college and career class during Sunday School," he announced.

"Teach?" I responded. "Teach the college kids? I can't do that. I can't teach my way out of a paper bag! They'd laugh me all the way to your office," I answered.

"Wait a minute, Jim," he said. "Don't you want the Lord to use you? Don't you trust him to prepare you?"

"Well, yes, but . . ." I fumbled.

He stopped me. "Jim, if *you* don't do it, somebody else will." I understood his words. God had a job that needed to be done. He was giving me a shot at it, and he intended for me to do it. What's more, he would help me do it. But if I refused, *I would be the loser!*

"I'll do it!" I told him. It was a tremendous blessing to me. I had the respect of the people, and even though I'm sure my first attempts were pathetically inept, God honored my willingness to try, and the class grew, both spiritually and in numbers.

I spent hours studying God's Word in preparation for those classes. I studied two or three hours every morning. It was during this time that I was attending more night classes at Moody Bible Institute, which helped me grow spiritually by leaps and bounds. I learned that I could become the man of God that God had planned for me to be.

During the time I was teaching, Belmont changed pastors. One day the new pastor came to me. "Jim," he said, "someday soon we're going to need an associate pastor here."

"That's great," I answered. "I'll be praying that God sends just the right man for the job."

"He already has," Pastor Cope replied. *"You're the man!"* He explained to me that a local Assembly of God Church is autonomous and can hire whoever it wants for its ministerial staff. Licensing with the denomination is not mandatory. I could be hired by the church as a full-time minister.

My heart burned in anticipation of being able to enter full-time ministry. I had been called by God to ministry while I was still at Teen Challenge, but I had never been able to see how that call could ever become a reality.

"How can I enter the ministry?" I had asked Barb many times. "I'm a man with a past, a man who's been divorced. With that past I can never be licensed as a pastor in the Assemblies of God, and that's the only denomination I've ever felt God wanted me to be a part of. Now I knew I could.

Barb had believed for several years that my goal would become a reality. When I couldn't see how God could bring it to pass, she remained firm in her belief that that was exactly what God could — and would — do. "Hey, aren't you the one with all the faith?" she'd tease. "If God called you, don't you think he's smart enough to know what he called you to, and when he wants you to begin?"

Late in 1978 soon after he talked to me, Pastor Cope announced to the church that he was planning to bring an associate pastor on staff. I sat in the congregational meeting fearfully awaiting his announcement. "I feel that God has already placed in our midst the man whom I want for my associate," he continued. "I believe that God wants Jim Dycus to be our associate pastor!"

The congregation unanimously agreed, and I was hired. I began late in January of 1979. I was so excited to begin that I got sick on the first day and had to go home. I was overwhelmed with the opportunity for ministry that God had given to me; I was determined to burn the place up for Jesus.

One of the first things I learned was that determination doesn't always make up for lack of experience. There must have been many times Pastor Cope wondered whether he had understood the Lord correctly when he chose me for his associate.

One morning when I came in the back door of the church, shouting my usual "Hallelujah!" to no one in particular, I heard him say, "Jim, could I see you for a minute?"

"Sure, Pastor Cope," I answered, walking into his office. He had a rather stern look on his face, but I just figured the drive in on the expressway must have been a hassle.

"How did your hospital visit with Susan go yesterday?" he asked.

I began to laugh. "Oh, Pastor, I think I really picked her spirits up," I said. "You won't believe what I did."

"Try me," he said, still looking rather serious.

"Well, I knew she was probably feeling pretty discouraged after her surgery," I explained, "so I decided I'd try to take her mind off her troubles. I wore a big rubber banana nose when I went in to see her." I broke out laughing as I remembered the effect that nose had had on Susan and her roommate.

Susan had looked terribly discouraged when I first looked in her door. But when she saw me walk in, she forgot her troubles and laughed. I remember how Ken had always kept the guys laughing at

Teen Challenge. "Jim, Jesus wants to make you happy. He wants you to enjoy living for him," he had told me.

Pastor Cope's voice brought me back to the present. I recognized that this wasn't one of those times for laughter. "Jim, I don't want you ever to make another hospital call wearing that rubber nose," he said.

I realized that he knew more than he was telling me. "What did I do wrong?" I asked, aware that I must have made a serious mistake.

"Susan called me after you left," he explained. "She told me all about your visit. She said that she and her roommate had laughed so hard that her roommate tore several stitches loose. The doctor had to take her back to surgery to reclose her incision!"

Not only was hospital visitation harder than I anticipated; so was sermon preparation. Even though I had prepared myself for this day with my night classes at Moody Bible Institute, I soon learned that preaching was harder than it looked.

One of the television evangelists that I most admired in my early days of salvation was Jimmy Swaggart. He was my favorite recording artist, and his music helped me through those difficult days after I left Teen Challenge to return to the Salvation Army. I also admired his preaching and dreamed of the day when I would become as capable of sharing God's message as he was. I practiced speaking in his tone of voice, using his gestures for accent, and strutting the way he did when he preached.

Finally the day came when I was prepared to go on the platform and present a message to the people of Belmont. I felt sure that I could deliver that Word from God as effectively as Jimmy Swaggart.

As I warmed up to my message, I began to move about the platform as I had seen Jimmy do. The only trouble was that I hadn't paid any attention to how he avoided getting all tangled up in the microphone cord! As I strutted back and forth, waving my Bible, I became more and more wrapped up in more than my sermon. Finally there was no cord left. I turned one last time and then stood there, hopelessly tied up in microphone cord. That was the last time I tried to be Jimmy Swaggart!

My early counseling wasn't any better. I always felt sympathetic toward the people who came to counsel with me—they usually came with heavy burdens—and I longed to be able to encourage them, help them overcome their hurts, and go on in the joy of the Lord.

One day I had an appointment with Janice, who was going

through a particularly difficult time during a divorce. I longed to be able to begin the counseling session on a positive note, to help her see that in the midst of her discouragement God could bring her joy. When it was time for her appointment, I put an oversized pair of rubber bare feet on over my shoes. At her knock on the door I stood up and walked around the desk to swing the door open.

"Hello, Janice, come on in," I began. Standing there in the hall was Pastor Cope—with a man I'd never met.

"Jim, I'd like you to meet our district superintendent," he said. Then, noticing my feet, he rushed through the introduction and hurried his visitor away toward his own office.

"Well, God," I prayed as I sank back into my chair, "there's more to this being a minister than I understand. Guess you've got an awful lot to teach this old boy off the streets of Chicago!"

Looking back now, I can understand that God would never take that spontaneity of laughter from me. He can use my unique, zany personality in his kingdom just as much as he can use someone quiet and reserved, like Barb and Paster Cope. In fact, he can bring a balance into all our lives as we allow him to mold us together in ministry and life.

I still enjoy making people laugh. I have my own "bag of tricks" in my office—the banana nose (along with many other kinds of noses), a big rubber thumb, a rubber chicken, and numerous other funny props that people have given me. I once heard Barb say to Jo, my secretary, "If Jim dies in his office, please get his 'bag of tricks' out of his desk drawer before Pastor Alex finds it!"

I cut up often, because I know that laughter is a window to the soul—and besides, that's me. And God allows me to be *me!*

It wasn't long before I realized that I needed to be credentialed in order to perform some of my ministerial duties. I knew what our denomination's policy was regarding the credentialing of a divorced man, but I decided to appeal to the Assemblies of God district superintendent anyway.

His reply came a few weeks later: "I don't know when, if ever, this matter will be changed by our denomination. My philosophy is that it is very difficult for the Lord to hold these matters against someone who didn't even know that the Lord, or his power or grace, existed. If I were you I would not let this matter grieve me to the point of ineffectiveness, but I would work diligently in the church, giving myself totally to the Lord in whatever ministry the pastor felt I would serve. . . ."

I was disappointed, but I felt the love and compassion of his reply and I determined to do just that—give myself totally to the Lord without allowing myself to become bitter or judgmental. I knew that bitterness would make me ineffective in ministry.

I became licensed, and ultimately ordained, through another organization. But my ministry was and is in the Assemblies of God. I recognized God's ability to open doors where man cannot. God called me to the Assemblies and he has placed me in ministry there, even though I'm not an ordained Assembly of God minister.

I hadn't been in the ministry long before something else began to happen. I had never in my Christian life felt different than anyone else because of my past. I had never suffered from rejection or the stigma of divorce until I became a minister.

But as I attended ministers' meetings, I experienced some rejection. There were usually three sign-in sheets at these meetings: one for "Ordained Pastors," another for "Licensed Pastors," and a third that read "Others." Many times, while the rest of the pastors lined up at the first two lists, I walked alone over to the "Others"!

My heart ached. I didn't feel like some fly-by-night preacher. I felt anointed and blessed by God to do what I was doing. Yet when meeting organizers asked for new ministers in the area to stand, I couldn't stand. It was humiliating for me at times.

I felt the same at ordination services that I attended. As men would stand and be ordained into ministry, the denominational leaders would pray for them, asking God's blessing on their ministry and laying their hands on them, anointing them for service.

"God, I want so badly to serve you, to be used by you. I want to give my whole heart and life over to you. I want to be completely motivated by you," I would pray. Then, in agony, I would continue, "I want more than anything to be licensed by the Assemblies of God. This is the denomination that you have called me to!" I cried. "Why can't this become a reality for me too?"

Our district superintendent encouraged me to try again. "Send me the details, Jim, and let's see what we can do."

My heart jumped with joy at the thought that it might be possible to become licensed. With great anticipation I wrote my response to him and awaited his reply.

"After reading your letter and the circumstances surrounding your marriages, I do not believe that you would qualify for the dissolutions as outlined by the General Council of the Assemblies of God," he wrote. But then, with a heart of love, he continued, "I have no reservations in using you for ministry in our district. You are deeply loved and accepted in our Fellowship, and nothing will ever change that! When God calls, he always provides a door of ministry, and in your case, it seems that he is opening many doors. Just follow his lead and you will not be disappointed."

Suddenly the issue was no longer important to me! I had been looking for acceptance in a piece of paper, yet God had already provided that acceptance, unconditionally, in the hearts of his servants. I was totally accepted, totally loved. And no piece of paper could ever make me feel more accepted or loved. The rejection and stigma that I had felt had been in my own mind. Once I let go of that rejection it was gone.

At least I thought it was!

One day I sat listening to the sermon of a man I deeply loved and respected. He was preaching on the sin of divorce. He related that it was against God's will and warned that we must be sure we never fail God in the area of divorce. I agreed completely with him. I knew firsthand the results of failure in divorce. But then, in order to stress his point, he said, "A divorced man will never pastor behind this pulpit!"

I knew he wasn't directing his remarks at me, but I was crushed. I felt like a condemned man. I felt no healing, no grace—just the load of guilt that I had felt for so many years before God had forgiven me.

I struggled again with my frustrations at being a divorced man trying to become an accepted minister. I was trapped by my past, imprisoned in shackles of stigma, and threatened with the destruction of all my hope of ever being any good to God.

I feel just like I did the night Lenny Slade was going to take me out! I thought as I listened to that preacher. I could even see Lenny's face as I stared up at the pulpit. Betrayed, I thought. He betrayed me! I felt as though the preacher's words had the power to destroy me.

I remembered how I used to reach in my pocket for the reassuring touch of the cold steel of my revolver. But this time I had nothing to fight with. Back then I knew how to defend myself; I was sure of my own strength. Now I was defenseless!

As I struggled one night with the aftermath of what his words had done to me, I cried out in prayer, "If I have the opportunity to preach the grace and forgiveness of God, I'll offer help and healing for the hurts that are already there. I want to do all that I can to provide some kind of ministry for the many divorced people who sit in congregations throughout this nation, feeling God's call on their lives but feeling restricted and bound by divorce," I promised God.

One night shortly after this I reached the pinnacle of despair and frustration. Near midnight I drove to the church, went into the sanctuary, and threw myself on the floor, face down in front of the altar.

"God, I've reached the end of my endurance," I sobbed out to him. "Either get me in the ministry, or get me out!" I didn't want to be half a minister with a whole burden any longer. I wanted him to either remove the burden or open the doors to let me do something great for God in the area of divorce.

"*Give me the divorced for my inheritance!*" I cried. "Let me be a role model of divine grace. Let me show the way to overcoming the frustrations of divorce. Let me prove your faithfulness to forgive and remove the penalty of sin in the area of divorce. Let me become a divorced hero for divorced people!"

18. A Single Focus

When I prayed that prayer face down in the sanctuary late at night, I had no idea how God was going to answer it. Or even if he would. But soon after that night God began to bring a focus to my ministry. I was still associate pastor at Belmont Evangelical Church. I still had responsibilities for hospital visitation, Christian Education, ministry to single persons, and many other things. But I felt a pull, a tugging in my heart to develop a ministry especially for the many separated and divorced people I had seen come into our church.

I knew their pain; I'd felt it too. And it wasn't easily erased. Too many times I'd watched them walk out of our church with the same pain-filled look on their faces as they'd had when they walked in.

I realized how important it was to reach them where they were, let them know that God understood and loved them and that there was a way to find healing for the hurts they had experienced. But it would take a special kind of ministry — one that offered support and fellowship for them, as well as encouragement to rise above their hurt into the new and different life God had for them beyond divorce.

God answered my prayer above and beyond my expectations. From the very first Divorce Recovery Seminar that I conducted soon after that night, he began to give me a vision of a ministry of support and guidance to divorced and separated people and their families. Barb worked with me in this area of ministry, fulfilling her call to full-time ministry once again. The very things that had been tools of the devil in my past became instruments of healing in my ministry. The hurts that I had experienced were able to make me compassionate and understanding about the hurts of others. The growth that God had initiated in my life became a pattern of growth in the lives of others.

As I prayed for guidance, God directed my thoughts to two special portions of his Word. First, through the story of the woman taken in adultery in John 8. As I read that story of a woman hurt and alone, God softly said to me, "See how my son met her need? He didn't condemn her as the others did; he didn't tell her that she would never be any good again. But he did tell her that in his presence was the power to live above her failure, to move into a life unhindered by her sin."

I recognized the principle that God was sharing with me. Divorced people *have* sinned. But their sin is no greater than the sin of any man or woman who has failed God in any area of life. And in the presence of God there is power to overcome the guilt and condemnation brought on by our sin. The issue is not whether people should or should not divorce. God's standards for marriage will never change. But the fact is that people *do* divorce. I needed to minister to them from that point on, as Christ had to the woman taken in adultery.

Then, as I read the story of the woman at the well of Samaria in John 4, again I heard God speaking to me: "See how I brought healing to that woman's life," he said. "I healed her totally, completely. I revolutionized her life. And then I sent her back to be a witness of my transformation. I gave her a calling to become an evangelist. That woman who had been divorced five times went back to her city to begin the first Divorce Recovery Seminar ever started."

I knew that's the message he wanted me to give to the divorced: that they could live effective, whole lives unhindered by mistakes of the past. Just as he had helped me to do.

His goal for his people in Jeremiah 29:11–14 became my goal for ministry to divorced and separated individuals: "For I know the plans I have for you . . . plans to prosper you and not to harm you, plans to give you hope and a future. Then you will call upon me and come and pray to me, and I will listen to you. You will seek me and find me when you seek me with all your heart. I will be found by you . . . and will bring you back from captivity. I will gather you from all the nations and places where I have banished you . . . and will bring you back to the place from which I carried you into exile" (NIV).

Divorce has held so many people captive to their hurts. Now God was calling me, allowing me to bring them back from their captivity so that he could reveal his plan for their lives. They could, they would, be healed.

From that time on Barb and I have been involved in this special ministry of compassion to divorced and separated individuals. We began ministering to the divorced who attended Belmont Evangelical Church. In the Divorce Recovery Seminars we helped them to understand the stages of divorce — the grieving, then the acceptance, and finally the ability to build new lives. We led them into seeing how forgiveness would open up the door for healing. We helped them to forgive themselves, to accept God's forgiveness, and to reach out with forgiveness to those who had hurt them most. We struggled together to diffuse the bomb of anger that so many hurt people have buried within and to learn to appropriate God's grace to let go of the past and move into the new life ahead.

God blessed our ministry, and the little group that we began with soon grew to over 200 people. Most of them were single parents who brought their children with them.

We provided babysitting for the kids. But sitter after sitter quit. "We just can't handle these kids," they would tell us.

I didn't know what to do. "God, how can we minister to the parents if they can't bring their kids? They can't afford babysitters of their own. What can we do to help?"

One night after a particularly disappointing evening with the kids, Barb and I discussed what to do as we drove home. "Barb, I'm afraid our ministry to the parents will be a failure if we can't solve the problem with the kids," I said.

She had no solution either. As we drove in silence, agonizing with the problem, I heard God speak again in the stillness — this time, in language I could understand. "Dummy, don't you see what I'm trying to show you?" I heard. "These kids don't need babysitters; they need ministry, just like their parents!"

I shared the revelation with Barb. "You'll have to try to find some way to teach them," I told her. "I am teaching their parents."

At first Barb was in a panic and didn't know what to do. But the more she prayed about it, the more God began to help her. She was a child of divorce, so she knew where she had hurt and how God had healed her. She began to develop her own materials, and with God's help, in time that vision became a reality. We published a complete curriculum for children of divorce and used it with great success in our ministry in Chicago. God was indeed doing a new work through us.

We started traveling to other churches, helping them develop a ministry to families who had experienced the hurts of divorce. In 1984 we traveled to Winter Park, Florida, to conduct a Singles' Seminar at Calvary Assembly. I had met the pastor, Alex Clattenburg, earlier in the year at a conference in California.

He had overheard a conversation I had with another pastor at the end of one of the California workshops. Later he stopped me, and we talked for almost an hour. He asked my goals, and the desires I had for my life and ministry. As I shared my vision with him, I sensed that he was more than casually interested in me.

"Are you asking me if I'm interested in coming to your church?" I asked. "Because if you are, you need to know that my vision is for Illinois. I'm not at all interested in leaving my church in Chicago."

Several months passed before I heard from Pastor Clattenburg again. Then we were asked to arrange and conduct the seminar at his church. Barb and I went with mixed emotions. We sensed that perhaps he intended to ask us to assume the single-adult ministry at his church. I was thrilled at his confidence in me, but I had no intention of ever leaving the city of Chicago. I love Chicago; it's been a part of me for all my life. My burden was to reach its lost for Christ.

At the end of the seminar he made a job proposal to me. I listened carefully to him, met his board, then boarded the plane to return to Chicago. I had promised to consider the offer, pray about it, and let him know. But I was already fully convinced that my answer would be no.

Yet something had happened. As I drove back down the familiar streets of Chicago, it looked like a new, strange city that I had never seen before. I felt empty, unchallenged, unmoved by the sights that had stirred my soul in previous days.

One night soon after our return I woke up out of a sound sleep at three o'clock in the morning. Nothing was moving; no sounds could be heard. Yet I was poised in expectation, every fiber of my being strained to hear. Suddenly I heard a voice speak: "It's over, Jim!"

Those three words quickened my spirit into a racing flow of thoughts. I knew that voice. I'd heard it before when it said, "Remember our deal."

I drove to the office the next day down North Avenue. It was a street I knew like the back of my hand. My mother had walked hand in hand with me on this street when I was a child. In my youth I had cruised the avenue in my car. I had copped drugs along it, held up drugstores that lined it—even been arrested here several times. And in my new life I had driven this street every day, praying as I did so that God would let me reach its people for him.

Today the street looked and felt different. I didn't know where I was. Unable to find familiar landmarks, I was totally confused by what was happening. As I sat in my office later, contemplating what was going on, the voice spoke again to me. "It's over, Jim. Your work here is over."

I knew immediately that it was God who had changed my perceptions. I knew that he had closed the door on my ministry in Chicago to open a door of ministry for me at Calvary Assembly in Winter Park, Florida. And I knew that someone else would complete the job in Chicago. God meant for the hurting in Chicago to find healing as I had. But he also meant for me to follow his directions, and begin to reach the hurting in Florida.

As I shared the news with Barb, told her about God saying, "It's over," she responded, "I know, Jim. We're going to Florida."

And we did. And God has continued to direct our singles' ministry in his own special way. I've discovered that even though God has completely removed the penalty of the past, eradicated its effect on my life, nevertheless he has used my past as the foundation for my future. My past has become a stepping-stone to my ministry today.

One day I sat across from a young single woman in our ministry. "Pastor Jim," she sobbed, "I don't know what to do. Can you please help me?" She was unmarried and pregnant, and there was no chance of the baby's father marrying her. She was guilt-laden, overcome by her sense of sin, and totally devastated.

As I listened to her cry for help, my mind flashed back to the girls who had worked for me in my old life. When one of them had come to me with an unwanted pregnancy, I had had no answers. My only help had been to send her, and others like her, to a crooked doctor for an abortion.

Today I have the answer: "Listen to what God can do for you," I counseled her. She accepted the challenge to place her dependence on God. Our singles' ministry reached out to her, loved her through her pregnancy, and adopted this beautiful single parent and her little child into its heart. Her dependence is on a God who has promised to be "a father of the fatherless" (Psalm 68:5, KJV).

In that same singles' ministry there is a host of single-parent families who need that promise, who depend on it. As they look to me, their pastor, to bring them hope, I am again reminded of the women and children whom I met in my old life. They ran from me, women hurrying children across the street to avoid coming into contact with me. But God has completely transformed me, and today I have hope to offer.

These single parents can become involved in our dynamic, exciting Single-Parent Family Institute. They can learn to live above their hurts in Crisis and Recovery workshops and can learn to live brand new fulfilled lives in the Life Management workshops. They can, with their children, be involved in ministry to others, proving the ability of a loving God to perform a miracle in their lives. More than 200 children alone have learned to live new lives, and several hundred parents have moved into this new life. Throughout the nation churches have begun to catch this vision and are effectively ministering to divorced and single-parent families.

My God has the power to turn our failures into his successes. Not long ago, I received a letter from a troubled, discouraged man. His was a familiar story, one I'd heard before: "Pastor Dycus, God has called me into full-time ministry. But because of a divorce in my past, *I know* that God will never to able to use me. I can't even get a license within my denomination."

Again my mind flashed back to the glorious time when I felt God's call on my life. *Me:* ex-drug addict, alcoholic, man with several divorces in his past—how could *I* be a minister?"

In my doubt and fear God had spoken to me through the example of Abraham. Like that man of long ago, I "staggered not at the promise of God through unbelief, but was strong in faith, giving glory to God; and being fully persuaded, that what he had promised, *he was able also to perform*" (Romans 4:20–21, KJV).

God has proven his ability to perform! He moved me through the open doors that he had prepared—doors that no human could have opened or shut. While the denomination to which God called me has not been able to ordain me to ministry, *God has!*

"God doesn't need the help of man to fulfill his call in your life," I wrote back. "But he needs *your* help. You must be willing to give God time to open the door for ministry to you. If he has called you, *he will get you in the ministry!* But he won't be able to do it if you become bitter or judgmental in your attitude toward others who cannot do it."

As I dropped that letter in the mail, I was again reminded of the encouragement and example that Ken had provided for me. He lived his life so completely surrendered to his Lord that he silently challenged everyone he met, and especially me, to come up to the same level of commitment.

That's my desire too. I want my life to show others that the sky's the limit with God. I want to be the example, lead the way for others who have suffered the same hurts as I have suffered to see that God can make success from failure.

I remember the story of Joan of Arc. When she had informed one of her generals that she would be leading the troops into battle, his response had been, "They won't follow you."

She had replied, "I'm going forward. And I won't be looking back to see who's following me."

I'm going forward too. I'm going to be the man God created me to be.

19. The Prodigal Parent Restored

"I'm home," I announced as I walked in the house from the garage.

"Daddy, Daddy, I love you!" our three-year-old, Dinah, yelled at the top of her lungs as she ran across the room and threw herself into my arms. As I lifted her up and swung her around, her tiny little arms gripped my neck as tightly as they could. I held her close, remembering the lonely years when holding my child in my arms was only a fantasy, and one that I felt could never become a reality.

God had answered my prayers for a family of my own. In fact, I'm reminded every day of that prayer I prayed before Barb and I had children. "God, give me a son just like me." Jimmy *is* just like me—for better or worse. As we give all our energies to raising this son, with his aggressive, domineering nature, his strong, energetic, combustible spirit, I sometimes wonder if I shouldn't have prayed for just a son. But God has assured us that if we do our part as parents to guide him while he's young, to bend the spirit to desire the will of God, this son of mine will be able to accomplish great things for the Lord in his manhood.

As I face this challenge daily, I often wonder what would have happened differently in my life if my father had done that for me. I've never doubted Dad's love for me in my childhood years, and I loved him. But that wasn't enough. Dad gave me his love, but he never earned my respect. He never took command of me; he didn't use his strength and authority with me. He let me dominate him rather than dominating and shaping me. And because he never controlled me, I never learned to control myself either.

I became a prodigal son and then a prodigal parent. I wasted myself and my youth on wantonness, just as the prodigal son did in Luke 15. But God has brought me back, given me a new life and a new family, and I'm determined that my children will have every opportunity to learn to give themselves in total commitment to the God who can bring them into the full potential of what he designed them to become.

But even though God has given me a new family, the ache has never left my heart for the children I lost. Barb and I often talked about those children. We prayed that sometime in the future God would bring my children back to me.

That ache was with me every time I counseled with a single parent whose child was struggling with the pain of losing the other parent. I felt the pain of men who sat before me sobbing because, having allowed a break in their relationship with their children, they now ached for restoration but couldn't make it happen. But most of all, the ache would burst forth into open pain when little boys without a dad would climb into my lap and say, "Will you be my daddy?" The tears would flow down my cheeks as their pain became my own. I'd cry for Dad, for the broken relationship we'd allowed to happen and that could never now be repaired. I'd cry for my own four children, lost because of my abdication of parenthood, and I'd cry with the pain of the little boy sitting on my lap, realizing that only God could make the miracle he longed for happen.

Then one day in 1983—we were still in Chicago—the miracle began to happen for me.

One day the telephone rang. When Barb answered, the voice on the other end asked, "Is this the home of Jim Dycus?"

"Yes, it is," she answered.

"Well, my name is Scott Dycus, and I think I'm your husband's son," the voice replied.

Barb knew at once that he was. We had talked about Scott often. We had had no idea how to contact him, but we knew that sometime, somehow, God would bring us back together.

Barb didn't want to spoil my joy. "My husband is a pastor here in Chicago. But he has a past that included a son. He may be your father. Why don't you call him at his office and find out?"

He said he would, and hung up. Barb sat there silently rejoicing in the reunion that she thought was taking place. Finally she could wait no longer. She called me at the office.

"How's your day going?" she asked. She tried to sound nonchalant, but I caught the excitement in her voice.

"Why do you want to know?" I asked.

"Well, did you get any interesting phone calls this morning?" she went on.

"No," I said.

"Oh," was her only reply.

By now I was tired of the cat-and-mouse game she was playing. "Okay," I pressed her, "who's going to call me?"

"Oh, just your son Scott," she answered, trying to be calm and cool.

My heart left my chest and rose up in my throat. I leaned back in my chair and didn't respond for a moment. Finally I found my voice and began to question her. She told me all about the phone call and said she was sure he'd call at any minute.

After we hung up, I sat quietly, my mind racing with the memories as well as the anticipation of what was about to happen. My son, my firstborn son, was going to call me! I had to mentally figure up his age: my baby son was now twenty-one years old. He was a *man,* a grown man! The same age as I was when he was born. I put my hand on the telephone, trying to hurry along the call.

He didn't call for six hours! He told me later that he had been trying to work up enough nerve to make the call. Meanwhile, I had been trying to work up enough nerve to answer his call.

But finally, by a miracle that God had arranged, I was talking to my firstborn son. Scott even called me Daddy. "Daddy, I don't want anything from you," he said that first day on the phone. "The only thing I've ever wanted was to know my dad. I just want to meet you, get to know you." He seemed to have no bitter feelings toward me, no hatred for the fact that I'd deserted him when he was only one month old.

Later that year he came to live with us. It was a glorious reunion as Barb and I and the kids met him at the train station. I was scared to death, having faced the possibility of that reunion many times in my mind. But until I actually stood there, physically waiting to see my son for the first time in over twenty-one years, I didn't realize how emotional the moment would really be.

"How will I recognize him?" I asked Barb. "How will he recognize me?" Barb devised a plan. She made a poster for our six-year-old son, Jimmy, to carry as he waited with us in the station. It read, "Where's my big brother, Scott?"

As we stood waiting for his train, my mind was filled with anticipation, fear, and suspense. "What if he doesn't want to be a part of my life? What if he hates me for what I did? What if this reunion doesn't work out?" The what-ifs plagued me until I was shaking with emotion.

At last the train pulled in. Jimmy moved up close to the door, and I stepped up behind him. We waited while every single person on that train filed past us. "Isn't there anyone else getting off?" I asked the conductor.

"No, sir, that was all of them," he answered.

"Well, my son is coming from Tennessee," I began.

"Sir, this train is from New York," he interrupted me. "The one from Tennessee will arrive over there, at Gate 6!"

Barb laughed, but I didn't think it was so funny. We moved over to Gate 6 and waited some more. Finally another train pulled in. Jimmy was so excited that again he moved up to the door with his poster. I was right behind him. Suddenly I saw Scott get off the train. I knew the moment I saw him that he was my son. He looked like me, walked like me—there was no doubt that he was mine!

He saw me and knew me instantly also. He walked off that train into my waiting arms, trapping Jimmy and his poster in the middle. We stood there many minutes, arms around each other. We were both overcome with emotion—father and son at last together.

"I love you, Daddy, I love you!" he sobbed in my ear.

One day during the several months he lived with us I asked him why he had no bitterness toward me. "Through all my life Mother kept telling me good things about you, Daddy," Scott told me. "She said you were a good man, just messed up—that you'd love me if you could, that you'd want me to be your son. She said that I looked like you and laughed like you, and that you'd be proud to know me as your son." And I am!

I'm still not sure why his mother said those positive things about me. There was nothing good about the way I treated her, the man I was back then. But she loved her son enough to rise above her own broken hopes and dreams and give him a dream. To let him have the hope of one day knowing his missing parent.

The time of restoration was a blessing to each of us. Jimmy idolized his big brother, and Scott loved our children. I had the special joy of leading Scott into a personal relationship with Jesus Christ as Savior and Lord of his life, and he got involved with us in church.

Scott stayed in Chicago when we moved to Florida. As I moved away from him in physical distance for the second time in my life, I prayed that God would continue to bring us closer together in a special father-son relationship. I also prayed for my other children

—Katie and Elaine, the little girls I'd left behind. I prayed that God would someday let me meet my other son, a boy I've never even seen.

The miracle of restoration wasn't complete yet, but God wasn't finished yet either. On the last day of September 1987 the phone rang again. I answered.

"Are you Jim Dycus?" a youthful, feminine voice asked. "Well, this is your daughter—Elaine!"

I heard a hesitancy, a sudden catch in her voice before she said her name. As she finished speaking, I stood silently for a moment while the crashing of a thousand painful memories began within my mind.

I shut my eyes and the shutters of my mind swung open. I was back in that lonely apartment on Waveland. No one was with me. As I looked around the room, I remembered every tormented moment I had spent there.

I looked into the hallway near the kitchen. They were still there—the crayon marks that Katie and Elaine had put along the wall were still there!

But this time I couldn't hear their happy laughter. There was only silence.

"Are you there?" Elaine's voice brought me back.

"Elaine—is it really you?" I asked. My heart was pounding. The emotions that I usually held so well in check began to rush over me. I groped for the side of the bed and sat down.

"Why didn't you ever try to reach me?" she asked accusingly. Seventeen years of confusion and bitterness at being deserted by her father rang out in her voice.

How could I ever explain? What could I say to this grown-up, eighteen-year-old daughter of mine whom I hadn't seen since she was a baby?

While we talked for nearly an hour, I relived each moment of agony that I had brought upon her mother. I listened as Elaine spilled out seventeen years of longing to know her father. And with the longing came the bitterness that my rejection had brought her.

"Elaine, I need to ask you to try very hard to believe what I have to say," I tried to explain. "There were many times when I wanted to find you. But I knew the immensity of torment that I'd put your mother through. I knew that any reappearance of me in her life, or yours, would only bring hurt—no healing."

"Don't you know how much pain you caused *me* by not looking for me?" she asked.

"Yes," I answered, "I understand pain!"

I told her some of my own pain. I told her of my mother's suicide, my father's death in the mental institution. I told her of the nightly parade of faces that had heaped guilt on guilt for all the pain I'd caused so many others. I told her of my bondage to that pain for fifteen years.

"But I'm a different man today!" I shared with her the miracle of transformation I had experienced when I gave my life to Christ in that Teen Challenge chapel in January of 1972.

"I can't change the past, Elaine. Everything you ever heard about me is true! The worst you heard was magnified in reality much worse than you knew. I was a bum; you were better off without me in your life. But God has been able to remove the guilt of my past, and he has given me the right to a new life!"

I heard the skepticism in her voice: "God never answered my prayer to bring you back!" she cried out, her voice breaking with heavy sobs.

"He's answering it right now, Elaine. It may have taken almost eighteen years, but he's answering your prayer right now." Suddenly a feeling of fear crept over me. "I'd like an opportunity to be a father to you now, Elaine," I began hesitantly. "That is, if it's what *you* want. Do you?"

It seemed a thousand years before I heard her reply: "Yes, I do!"

I shook with relief, and the tears flooded down my cheeks. "Then this can be the beginning of a new chapter in our lives," I told her.

As I hung the phone up, I lay back on the bed, overcome with the flood of emotions that Elaine's call had awakened within me.

Suddenly the bedroom door swung open and Dinah ran over to me. She crawled up on the bed and onto my chest, then laid her head down on me.

"I love you, Daddy," she said with all the happy spontaneity of her little heart. We lay there silently for many minutes. I wrapped my arms around her, praying that someday I would have the opportunity to wrap my arms around my two older daughters, Katie and Elaine.

When Dinah had had enough silence, she began to sing:

> If I had a penny or a nickel,
> I'd buy that poor doggie a bone.
> And I'd bring that doggie back to our house.
> And I'd give that doggie a home.

Her song struck a chord deep within me. "That's it, God!" I prayed. "That's what you did for me. You bought me out of my bondage to pain and guilt with the blood of your own Son. You brought me back to your house, and you gave me a home."

All at once I felt so safe. Even though it seemed that my past was moving into my present, I didn't fear. *Because I don't live in the past any longer!* I belong to God. I live the new life he birthed within me. I am *his!*

Only what God allows of my past can inhabit this new life. As my past walks into this new life that belongs to God, I'm given the privilege of seeing that broken, pain-filled past succumb to the miracle gift of transformation.

I still haven't held my two older daughters in my arms; the work of restoration isn't yet complete. But I've talked to both Katie and Elaine several times on the telephone, and we're moving into a restored father-daughter relationship.

The important thing is that God has opened the door! I couldn't do it. I could only live in the bondage of guilt caused when I slammed the door shut many years ago.

But God can set the captives free! The bondage of a broken past has been transformed into the miracle gift of a hopeful new life!

John 5:24 says it so well: "I tell you the truth, whoever hears my word and believes him who sent me has eternal life and will not be condemned; *he has crossed over from death to life*" (NIV).

Glossary of Drug Terms

Acid	Lysergic acid diethylamide (LSD-25)
Bag	Drug purchase
Bread	Money
Burned	Cheated or hurt by someone
Bust	Arrest
Catch one's lunch	Get beaten up or killed
Cold turkey	Sudden drug withdrawal
Connection	Go-between in a drug buy
Copping	Bartering or negotiating for a drug buy
Dead city	No action, boring existence
Dealer	Drug supplier
Dime bag	$10 purchase of narcotics
Dollies	Dolophine
Dope	Narcotics
Dopie	Drug addict
Downers	Depressants
Drive	Tingling sensation of pressure after injection
Dropping pills	Swallowing pills
Dynamite	Good, pure narcotics
Fix	Injection of narcotics
Gee	A short piece of dollar bill used to wrap a needle and dropper together for an injection
Goofballs	Barbiturates
High	Under the influence of drugs

Hit	Injection of drugs
Hooked	Addicted
Hustle	Engage in illegal activity to obtain drugs or money
Jack	Needle for a syringe
Joint	Marijuana cigarette
Joy-popping	Intramuscular (not intravenous) injection of drugs
Junk	Narcotics, heroin
Kick	Abandon drug habit
Mainline	Inject drugs directly into vein
Mind habit	Mental addiction remaining after a physical dependence is broken
Nickel bag	$5 purchase of drugs
Nod out	Doze after using drugs
O.D.	Overdose
Outfit	Paraphernalia used to inject narcotics: needle, dropper, spoon, and so on
Pimp	Man who has prostitutes working for him
Pot	Marijuana
Pusher	One who sells narcotics
Red devils	Seconal capsules
Rip off	Cheat or steal from
Rush	Sudden sensation after injection, usually felt mostly in the head
Scarf	Swallow drug pills
Score	Finalize a drug purchase
Set-up	Prearranged drug buy by police in order to arrest the one set up
Shake-down	Police search
Shooting gallery	Place where addicts go to inject drugs

Smack	Heroin
Strung out	Addicted or high on narcotics
Take off	Inject drugs
Take someone out	Beat up or kill someone
Tracks	Needle marks and scars on arms and legs
Tray	$3 purchase of drugs
Turning tricks	Prostituting
Uppers	Amphetamines, stimulants
Withdrawal	Physical symptoms from sudden drug withdrawal
Yellow jackets	Nembutal, a barbiturate capsule